I've Been Shot!

Encountering Christ in Trauma

Second Edition

Terrie Bentley McKee

For Greg, my husband, my hero, my soul-mate.
I love doing life with you.

For Sam, for time well spent
For Jacob, for your heart
For Elli, for your unconditional love
For Laura, for your Holy Spirit-filled sweetness with
a touch of sass and silliness
For Allyssa, for your calmness, joy, and peace

For the Charlotte Rollin' Hornets and Wheel Serve

For Pop and Mama B

Dedicated to Pastor Chris Howell

Kammie, Mike, Taylor, Morgan
John, Becky, Jena, Anna, Trent

In Memory of My Mother
Martha Breneman Bentley
January 25, 1941 – October 1, 2020

This book is solely written to glorify the Name above
all names: Jesus Christ our Lord, and to share the
Hope we have in Him with others.
Jesus is the only Way.

Contents

Chapter 1   Hemmed in, Behind and Before   9

Chapter 2   The Deafening Quiet   29

Chapter 3   A Choice to be Made   47

Chapter 4   Why Do Bad Things Happen   56
               to Good People?

Chapter 5   Sadness of Heart   67

Chapter 6   The Day is Almost Here   69

Chapter 7   The Lord Builds the House   83

Chapter 8   Whatever Situation   94

Chapter 9   Expecting   122

Chapter 10   Home for Christmas   135

Chapter 11   Through the Roof   143

Chapter 12   That My Heart Will Sing Your Praises   152

Chapter 13   Remember   162

Chapter 14   Addendum   173

               About the Author   184

Chapter One
Hemmed in Behind and Before

"The Lord himself goes before you and will be with you; he will never leave you nor forsake you. Do not be afraid; do not be discouraged."
Deuteronomy 31:8

I have dealt with special needs during all my years as a mother: in public, trying desperately to get my disabled son services and encouraging other parents dealing with the lonely world of autism; in private, barely keeping it together as the tantrums grew in proportion to his body. I've asked God *"Why?"* so many times in Sam's 23 years. *"What good can autism have?"*

Sam's autism made it extremely difficult to teach him about God. Santa Claus, you can see, touch, hear, talk with one-on-one at the mall. God can't be seen. You can't touch Him. Hearing His voice is sometimes difficult—especially when the noise of life interrupts. Helping Sam understand about God started out with us praying for people in ambulances as they sped past us, sirens blaring. Teaching Sam in concrete ways about God built his own faith and solidified mine. Still, in desperately terrible moments, Sam will still ask God, *"Why can't I be normal like other people?"*

Why questions tend to pull us down in the muck and mire where we are trapped by comparing ourselves to other people's mud holes in which *they* are trapped. *Why* questions expose discontentment in some form: *Why can't we have a bigger house--we have six people living in this one! I need a dog! Oh.My.Word! Shiplap!*

It took the events of November 28, 2015 and afterwards to make me realize that contentment is rooted in Christ alone. I learned that contentment breeds surrender, and surrender leads to submission.

Whoa. Dirty word, that. *Submission.* It conjures up images of slaves and bowing down to masters. *Yes. Exactly.* When we learn that Christ *is* our Master, and we are as slaves to Him, not out of fear or force but out of love and gratitude--it changes our whole mindset about submitting to Him, for the sake of our walk with Him and the witness we have of Him to others. Our walk takes on a kingdom-focus, Christ-centered point of view. In the middle of tragedies, though, it is hard to think about such things.

On the morning of November 28, 2015, the Saturday after Thanksgiving, my husband Greg, son Jacob, daughter Laura, and I were wrapping up our holiday project at his parents' home in Lynchburg, Virginia. It seems like every trip to their house has a project invested in it, and that's okay. We enjoy helping them; they help us when they visit. This time, we had worked with his parents and brother to clean, declutter, and reorganize the basement to make more livable space for them. As we sorted boxes and reminisced about things we found, five hours away in Charlotte, North Carolina, a black car pulled up at a 23-year-old woman's house. Keyona looked outside and saw that her boyfriend's friend Terrell and his wife were sitting in the driveway, waiting on her boyfriend Darren to finish his

cigarette while he sat on Keyona's front porch. He
finished and power-walked to the car.

While his wife was driving, Terrell told Darren of
the plan: drive up to Hillsborough and meet a man
to get money, go back and hang out with Terrell's
cousin in Greensboro, then come back to Charlotte.
Both Terrell and Darren were convicted felons;
Darren, who hadn't hit the six-week post-release
mark from prison yet, was carrying a silver .360
revolver in his pocket. He sat in the car during the
four-hour drive to Hillsborough, texting Keyona the
whole time. The plan was a drug deal.

About four in the afternoon, we waved goodbye to
Greg's family, and started our long five-hour drive
back home to Gastonia on the southwest side of
Charlotte. Driving through Greensboro two hours
into the trip, we chatted with Jacob about being on
Western Carolina University's marching band that
semester. As a freshman music major, he was excited
and thrilled about marching with his tenor sax.

Laura talked non-stop to herself. At five years old, she was listening to her Bubby's excited jabber but was more interested in what she, herself, had to say. So she looked outside despite dusk settling in, and talked to the window.

The talk after dinner focused on catching Jacob up on how our oldest son, Sam, was doing in the group home for people with developmental delays, and how Elli, Greg's daughter, was doing in her last year of high school in Pennsylvania.

At 7:30 in the evening, a man walked into the rest stop in Cabarrus County on I-85 Southbound. Traffic was light and the other guests were leaving in their cars. The custodian, who was preparing his cleaning cart for his last rounds, saw the man come in, spit into the water fountain, and go to the restroom. Disgusted, the custodian took out a spray bottle of bleach water and wiped out the water fountains. As he rinsed the bowl with water, he used the bleach water rag to wipe and polish the whole fountain, scrubbing off all the fingerprints that had dulled the shiny chrome.

The man walked out of the restroom and left the facility, getting into his vehicle. The custodian watched him walk out; as the doors opened, he saw two new guests smoking outside in the chilly November air, beside the automatic doors. The bigger of the two men had dreadlocks and was wearing a baggy white shirt and jean shorts. The shorter had dreads down to his waist, pulled back under a floppy hat. He was wearing a red and white shirt under a jacket. The custodian just figured, like most people traveling on I-85 Southbound, that they needed to stretch their legs. Still, those were some long dreads...

Traveling down I-85 Southbound, we talked about the special church service planned for the next morning. Our church had planned a Concert of Prayer for the two services that Sunday, with the first service starting at 8:30 a.m. and again at 11. We were excited about participating in a service dedicated just to prayer. In this tender moment, I shared with Greg something the Lord had laid on my heart: that He was about to bless us. Greg agreed; he had experienced that encouragement as well.

Continuing down the interstate, we laughed over fun family memories, like going to theme parks. Laura stopped talking; her interest was piqued: she asked questions about princesses and castles and we all answered them, smiling and laughing as we shared stories.

Traffic was amazingly light that evening so we made good time heading home from spending the holiday in Virginia. The sweet tea from dinner sneaked up on us and we soon needed a restroom break. Driving down I-85, we were in Concord, and Greg turned off the interstate into a rest area parking lot.

It would be the last time he drove the SUV. There were two buildings at this particular rest area: one for the restrooms, and the other for vending machines. Jacob went ahead into the restroom building and I followed, with Greg and Laura bringing up the rear, holding hands and chatting. I noticed a man walking from the vending building; he had an incredibly distinctive walk--a powerful swagger as though he owned the place. As a writer who notices such things, I took note of it. I looked ahead and there was another man, shorter than the first, with moles all over his face and a floppy hat on his head, with long dreadlocks pulled back. As it was getting chilly in the twilight hours, I didn't think much more about it, and went to the ladies' room.

Greg waited in the lobby with Laura; I came out and took her into the ladies' room. After she finished and washed her hands, we joined Jacob in the lobby. Greg was in the men's room. I decided to let Laura run around outside to burn off some energy, so the three of us walked through the door and past those two guys.

The brick patio right outside of the door was in a courtyard of sorts, with concrete squares surrounded by red bricks that formed diamond shaped-paths. Jacob chased Laura, saying, "I'm gonna get you! I'm gonna get you!" She giggled as she skipped along the paths.

I smiled while watching Jacob and Laura play. Having a funny feeling, I looked up. The two guys were watching us intently. They watched my daughter skip on the brick paths. Their eyes followed Jacob as though they were sizing him up. I didn't like the feeling I had, and called Laura back to me as she was skipping too far to my right.

The guys looked at me then at the door. Again, they looked at me and my children. After a head nod to each other, they turned with deliberation and walked inside the building. I sighed and rested a little easier: at least they weren't watching my kids.

Just a few moments later, a single, deafening shot pierced the solitude. Time moved so fast and so slowly at the same time. We started walking quickly toward the restroom building as the two guys sprinted out the door and past us. It did not process at that second what was going on.

"Help me!" I heard my beloved scream through the open door. "Help me!"

The three of us ran inside. Greg was on his belly in the men's room doorway floor, blood gushing from his nose. A pool of blood was under his face. "I've been shot!" he screamed.

There are moments in your life in which you don't even recognize your own voice. A primal, guttural scream launched from the depths of my soul: "No!" In the same moment, I looked at Jacob. We had understood, at the same exact time, what had happened: Those two guys, who had watched us outside, had shot Greg.

Jacob turned on a dime and bounded outside. Screaming at the guys who we could not see, he tried to bolt after them. I was right behind him, hearing Greg screaming, "No, Jacob! They will kill you!" Somehow, I grabbed Jacob's muscular body and threw him back towards the doors.

"Call 911!" I screamed at Jacob as I ran to the custodian's office. I screamed at him, "Please! My husband's been shot! Call 911!" I then realized he was, in fact, on the phone with the emergency dispatcher.

Greg was on his belly, blood still coming from his nose and pooling on the floor under his face. "Get my wallet," he said, reaching under himself and pulling the car keys from his jeans pocket; they slid across the floor.

I took his wallet from his back pocket and picked the keys off the floor. It then dawned on both of us: *they didn't take anything*. Greg had come out of the stall and was washing his hands at the sink. The two guys came in and stood on either side of him as he stood, washing his hands at the basin. By their actions, the men were herding him toward the sink and away from the doorway. The tall one with the powerful stride pulled a gun and pointed it at Greg's head. No words had been said. Fight-or-flight took over: Greg turned and bolted for the door; three zig-zagging steps, then: *bang!* He had immediately collapsed on the floor, all three-hundred pounds of him, face first–too fast to even bring his arms up to catch himself. He hit so hard the floor tiles cut into the bridge of his nose and between his eyebrows. While a little blood was on the back of his shirt surrounding the hole, all the blood that had pooled under him came from those tile imprints.

He had been shot in the back from three feet away.

It was a kill shot.

Laura was sitting on the floor, holding her legs with her arms and rocking back and forth, tears streaming down her face. Over and over she began to cry out: "My Daddy's dead, my Daddy's dead!"

"I'm not dead, Princess!" Greg yelled out, desperately trying to reach her through words when he could not physically get to her. "Daddy's not dead! I'm right here!"

I picked her up and she held me tight, crying. Greg called to me, steadying himself: "Terrie, I cannot feel my legs."

"Noooo!" screaming, crying, holding Laura, I cried out, "Jesus, have mercy!"

At that moment, a man came in the rest area lobby and saw the situation. "What happened?" he exclaimed. "Are you okay? What can I do to help?" We heard sirens through the closed door, coming from the interstate.

"Hold her!" I handed this total stranger my daughter, who hugged him. Laura was not one to go with strangers, but she willingly reached for this man. He walked the floor with her, asked her name, and rocked her as she sobbed on his shoulder. It was a strangely peaceful scene in the midst of the chaos.

Jacob, finished with the phone call, knelt down beside Greg. "What can I do?" he asked, kicking his lifeguard first-aid training into gear. Greg asked about the entrance wound. Jacob accessed the situation: there was a hole in the back of his shirt, a little blood around the hole in the shirt, but no exit wound.

Any other time, if Greg would get cut and see his own blood, he would pass out within three and a half minutes. This time--*Jesus.* Greg did not pass out at all, though he was staring at a growing pool of blood.

He had the presence of mind, while I was on the phone with his mother and losing what sanity I had, to access himself: airway, check. Breathing, yes. Cardio: pulse is there.

Laying on the floor, Greg prayed, "Lord, just let me take care of my family." The presence and peace of Christ was immediately upon him, as though Jesus hunkered down on the floor right next to him. *I gave you a desk job two years ago for this purpose. You have breath in your body.*

Greg looked at his arms, outstretched, and the puddle of blood under his face. *My body was broken, My blood was shed...*Greg heard Christ's gentle voice. In that moment, he understood: "he was pierced for our transgressions, he was crushed for our iniquities; the punishment that brought us peace was on him, and by his wounds we are healed," [Isaiah 53:5 NIV].

A lone tear fell as Greg silently thanked Jesus.

Two state troopers ran in the building, and while one knelt beside Greg, the other kept everyone inside and secured the building. He started asking us all questions. The one kneeling took notes as Greg gave him detailed descriptions, which the trooper relayed to other officers via radio. We heard the whirling buzz of police helicopters above the building as paramedics came in with a gurney and started administering aid to Greg.

In a blur of activity and tears, Greg was loaded up on the gurney. Headed out the door, he turned to me: "Terrie, I love you. I'm okay. Be safe on the way to the hospital."

I collapsed on the floor, ugly crying. Jacob picked me up and held me. Tears were actively flowing down my boy's cheeks. The man holding Laura stroked the back of her head as she silently cried.

As we walked outside with the trooper that had been asking questions, we were flooded by the red lights of the ambulance intermingled with the lights from police cruisers flying up the rest area drive.

As the paramedics were trying to get an IV in Greg in the ambulance, I confirmed with the trooper that he was being transported to the main hospital in Charlotte. The trooper looked at me, my face streaked with tears, and looked at Jacob.

"Can you drive?" the trooper asked Jacob.

"Yes!" exclaimed Jacob with confidence. "How do you get to the hospital?"

The trooper didn't try too hard to suppress a grin. He asked me the same question. "Yes," I said. "I have to do something." The trooper nodded; he understood. He walked over, hugged me, and said he was praying.

I reached out for Laura, who flung herself on me from the stranger. I thanked him profusely and asked his name. All I heard was "Elroy."

The youth pastor of our church, Chris, met us in the emergency department waiting room about ten minutes after we arrived. His daughter was with him and took charge of Laura. We couldn't see Greg as the ER team was working on him and accessing the damage. Finally, after what seemed like hours but was really only about thirty minutes, we were called to the private family room.

A detective greeted us and started asking questions. Jacob and I answered each one, giving descriptions of the two guys. Chris was in the room, praying and providing emotional support. The door opened and a triage doctor walked in and sat down.

He explained that the .380 caliber bullet entered Greg's spine at the first lumbar vertebrae and, due to the heat and velocity of the point-blank shooting, it had cauterized going in; it was basically welded in the bone. His spinal cord was severed. Bullet fragments were actively floating in the spinal fluid. Greg was paralyzed from the waist down.

The doctor paused as I slid off the little sofa and onto the floor, quietly sobbing, tears streaming down my face. Jacob's hands covered his face; his chest was heaving with sorrow and anger. The detective took notes, quickly but quietly. The scratch of his pencil to the pad was the only sound in the room.

"If the bullet," the doctor continued gently, "Had been a half-inch off in any direction, he would have been killed. There would have been too much internal damage."

Jesus. I knew in that moment, that those two guys may have pulled the trigger, but it was *Jesus* who had placed the bullet *precisely* where it would not kill him. He was severely injured--but he was not dead.

"Can you do surgery on him?" I asked.

"I don't think surgery is planned," the doctor said gently. "But that is up to the neurosurgeon who will be looking at him."

"Can I see him?"

"He's being moved in a few minutes to the trauma intensive care unit upstairs. I'll let you know when he's there." The doctor looked at the detective, then at Jacob. "I'm very sorry." He walked out.

The detective said that he had a few more questions, but they could wait. "I'll give you a little while," he said. "Please let me know if you need anything." He left the room.

Jacob went in the hallway to make phone calls. As he walked out, family friends, one of Greg's co-workers, and church members began to join us. I updated them until the doctor said we were allowed upstairs.

We waited while the detective was visiting Greg, praying and gathering up strength in Christ. As soon as allowed, I went back to the TICU to see him. I heard his screams down the hall and entered the room weeping, scared at what I was going to find. His eyes were wide, like a wounded animal, his head moving from side to side. "Oh dear God!" he yelled out, tears actively flowing down his cheeks as a nurse worked on getting a second IV line in. His nose and between his eyebrows were cut; his face was stained with blood.

"Oh, it burns, it burns!" he screamed. Nurses and doctors were buzzing about the room. "Oh Jesus," he cried out, tears streaming down his pain-stricken face. He then did the remarkable: raising one paper-bagged hand, all the way up, he screamed out, "Praise you! Praise you in this storm! You are God, You are Savior, praise You, praise You in this storm!"

Chapter Two
The Deafening Quiet

"Then the Spirit lifted me up,
and I heard behind me a loud rumbling sound
as the glory of the Lord rose from the place
where it was standing."
Ezekiel 3:12

⁊

Greg fought incredible pain throughout the night and into the early morning hours. Helpless, I sat in the world's most uncomfortable recliner in his TICU room and prayed. The heavy silence in the room, deafening against the minute beeps of the IV machine, added to the urgency of prayers.

Our friends had taken Jacob and Laura home. Nurses and techs came in quietly, took vitals, changed IV fluids, drew blood. I updated friends and family on social media, walked down the hall, crying and praying--it was as though someone was continually kicking me in the gut, which felt raw and empty, though no appetite for food was to be had.

I cried out to Jesus. Suddenly, His presence surrounded me. It was as though He was hugging me as we sat on a leather bench in the hallway. "Lord Jesus," I said aloud. "The house, the car, his job...what are we going to do? We have to get everything ready for a wheelchair..." Sighing, I whispered, "Lord, I don't know how...but I trust You. Jesus, Lord, You are sovereign."

Back in the room, Greg was holding his hand up, mouth moving in silent praises to Jesus in the electrical storm of nerves misfiring and shutting down. While he praised God, I dove into my black-leather Bible, gobbling up the Word. It was as though the Holy Spirit was moving the pages for me, leading me to just the perfect passages.

When I needed comfort, He led me to the Psalms. When fear would take my breath away, He led me to verses that started "do not be afraid," over and over again. When I felt vengeful toward those two men, he led me to Hebrews 10:31. "It is a dreadful thing to fall into the hands of the living God," [NIV].

I gasped, closing the Bible. Looking up at Greg's outstretched arm, his lips moving in silent prayers and tears cascading down his cheeks, I slid to the floor in awe, lifting the two men in prayer: *they have woken the Lion of Judah.*

Darren and Terrell had jumped in the car, which was had been waiting for them behind the vending machine building where no one walking on the courtyard could see. They had sped off into the darkness and roared down I-85. They made it to Keyona's house in record time; Darren had jumped out and the car roared out of her neighborhood. Hungry for the food Darren had promised, Keyona had met him at the door. "Where's my food!?" she had shouted.

Agitated, he had walked up and down the hallway. She asked him repeatedly what was wrong. "I done something," he had said. "I need you to hold this for me."

Thinking it was his cell phone by the weight and shape of it, she had taken it from his hands. "But where's my food?!"

"Woman, I didn't get you no food!" he had shouted. "I shot a man!"

She had gasped and looked down at her hand--she was holding the clip from a gun. Keyona threw it at him and cussed him out for coming in her home with her children like that. She reminded him that both of them were convicted felons, couldn't have guns...he had paced back and forth, sat down, stood up. She told him to leave, to call someone to come get him.

Swarms of police officers and crime scene investigators had the rest area on lock-down. K9 units searched the woods behind the rest area; their barking was muted by the sounds of police helicopters in the air above the trees, searching with spotlights.

Inside, the state trooper who had talked with Jacob and I about driving had cordoned off the men's restroom and the water fountain with crime scene tape. He had talked with the custodian, who had said moments before the family arrived, the shorter of the two men had used the water fountain that he had just cleaned. Crime scene investigators were busy, taking pictures and dusting for prints.

News crews arrived on scene as the police presence was dying down but still impressive. Several cruisers had blue lights circling from the tops of the police cars. A video camera in the vending machine building was spotted; they worked on making the surveillance footage available to the media.

In Gastonia, Sam was in his pajamas but up, getting ready to watch the 10 o'clock news with the other group home residents. It was a nightly ritual that he, frankly, didn't like. Except for the weather. He liked the weather.

Suddenly, the dramatic introductory music ended and Sam saw a picture of his step-dad on the television. "Horror in Concord tonight: a father of four has been shot at the Cabarrus County rest area..."

Sam suddenly stood, his mouth agape. Three group home staff ran to him as he dropped to his knees, screaming, sobbing, and hitting the floor with his fist.

There were so many questions with no answers. Would Greg have surgery? Could they extract the bullet? Would he ever walk again? How do we help the police capture the guys that did this?

Sitting on that bench beside the window, I looked outside at the dark of night. Tears streamed down my cheeks. We had been through so much over the last seven hours, and it was only three in the morning. Trying to process it all became a nightmare. It was too much. It was just too much.

I opened my Bible to the first chapter of Job. A servant ran to him: oxen and donkeys carried off, all but one servant killed. Job doesn't have the chance to respond when another servant runs to him: Chaldeans raided and carried the camels off and killed all but that servant. You can almost see Job grabbing his chest in horror: my poor servants! My livestock!

Then, "while he was still speaking, yet another messenger came and said, "Your sons and daughters were feasting and drinking wine at the oldest brother's house, when suddenly a mighty wind swept in from the desert and struck the four corners of the house. It collapsed on them and they are dead, and I am the only one who has escaped to tell you!" (Job 1:18-19 NIV).

"While he was still speaking." Job didn't have time to process what had happened to his before he was dealing with something else. My breath caught, reading the words "your sons and daughters." I could see Job's knees collapse and, reaching for the ground, sit hard in the dust at the mention of his ' children. He tore his robes in pain and anguish.

Clothing wasn't torn but I certainly walked the halls in pain and anguish, holding on to the handrail on the wall and crying. Shocked and bewildered, I didn't know what to do--except kneel in front of that leather bench, not caring if nurses or doctors looked at me weird, praying His Name, repeating "Jesus," again and again. Saying His Name became a stand-alone prayer.

Sleep was impossible. Sitting on the recliner in the room, I pulled out my laptop and prayed the sketchy wireless signal would hold. There, on a social media site, was a report from a news channel with video footage of the tall man with the powerful walk. He was walking in the aisle in the vending building. Striding. Swaggering. I hit *share*.

"Lord Jesus," I prayed, closing the laptop. "I can't forgive these men in my own power, only in you. Please forgive them and lead them into a relationship with you. Help the police find them."

Cold, I wrapped myself up in a blanket the nurse gave me and tried to rest; I was exhausted from crying and processing. In the darkness, Greg's moans paused as he asked, shivering, "Is the room cold to you?" Getting up and looking at the thermostat on the wall, I told him that it was reading 70 degrees, but I'd ask the nurse for another blanket. She brought two, and Greg told me to try to sleep, using one of the blankets. Even in the state he was in, he was putting me first. He was the same Greg. Comforted beyond my ability to describe it, I laid back in the recliner and rested.

The nurse had finally been given the orders to give Greg a cocktail of powerful pain medications that would certainly allow him to sleep. She came in at 4:30, pushed the meds through the IV and followed it with saline. He fell asleep quickly, and I dozed off.

Far too soon, sunlight pierced through ripples in the blinds and I woke up. Getting out of the recliner to use the restroom, I looked at the clock: 8:15. Shivering, I checked the thermostat: 70 degrees. The prayer service would be starting soon.

At 8:35, Greg whispered, "Terrie?"

I asked from the recliner, "What is it?"

"The prayer service has started," he said. "Jesus... is here." The room was noticeably warmer, though no one had touched the thermostat in the 20 minutes before. I got up and walked to the thermostat--73 degrees.

I knelt beside the bed and held Greg's hand. We both quietly prayed along with our brothers and sisters at Flint Groves Baptist, as they were praying for us. There was a holy, peaceful presence in the room as the prayers of the saints drifted to heaven like incense in the temple.

Greg's parents, Gary and Barbara, texted: they were on their way. Greg was in and out of consciousness from the pain medication. Watching him sleep, I thought about the events of the last several hours.

There's something incredible about unrelenting, overwhelming stress that made my belly raw and kicked-in. It comes with the territory of having a child with autism, but until the shooting, I never had to deal with something of that magnitude. *The senselessness* of it all--that word kept coming back to me. *They didn't take anything.* I didn't even have a chance to talk with Greg about what happened in the restroom, with him in so much pain and then medicated. The stress of trying to juggle all these balls in the air--Greg's pain management, the future, what happened, the kids...myself... The question kept coming up: how do people who do not have faith in Jesus Christ deal with trauma on this magnitude?

I clung to Jesus, slept with my Bible, hearing His sweet voice wash over me through scripture. *Do not fear...for I am with you.* Thinking about the car ride here, I remembered us talking about the Lord blessing us. Feeling Jesus' presence, hot tears etched down my cheeks. *I am the Lord your God...I am the Resurrection and the Life...*the pain in my gut was suddenly changed into a breathless understanding: Jesus *is* the blessing.

In today's world, especially because of the false prosperity gospel, we tend to think blessings come in the form of financial wealth, good health, or well-behaved children. This is not what the Bible teaches. The Bible says that though we may be poor financially, we can be rich in Him. Though we may be ill or injured, we can be whole in Him. Though we may not have ideal family situations, He is still the Good Shepherd. Because of Jesus, we can sail through the fleeting troubles of this world with an understanding that we are just traveling through this place. Real, tangible blessings come from Christ, and the biggest blessing of all is Jesus alone.

Throughout the Scriptures, God reminded Israel of their deliverance in Egypt. Why did He remind them of that incredible, miraculous event time after time? *Because they kept forgetting.* Two years before the shooting, during a mission trip to Africa, God kept placing the phrase "I am the Provider and the Provision" upon my heart. That was alive to me in Africa as I met African bush women who lived in mud huts and had two pots in which to cook, yet, they had said, because they had Jesus, they were rich beyond measure.

God reminded me of the time years before, struggling with an abusive husband in my first marriage then in the financial uncertainty of being a single mom, He provided food on my doorstep at the exact moment we needed it. He was my calm and the peace of my boys. Kneeling before that bench in the hallway, God reminded me that He is the same God Who provided then—why would He stop?

Walking back to Greg, Christ reminded me that He is the Provider and the Provision in that beeping hospital room. Though we had no idea how we were going to pay for Greg's lengthy hospital stay, or house renovations, or what the future would hold, Christ's presence in that place signaled that He was in this with us. We needed to remember how He was with us in the past to know that He would be with us in the future, and no matter what that looked like, it was going to be okay.

Sitting there, praying and just talking with Jesus, I thanked Him for the provision that was not yet tangible. After sitting in silence, wondering if I should say it, I realized He already knew my thoughts: so I spoke, and told Him I was angry. Angry at the men who shot my husband. Angry at how they have changed all our lives, forever. *I know,* my soul heard my Shepherd say. *Trust Me...*

❧

Throughout the New Testament, Jesus tells His followers that they must die to self. "Whoever wants to be my disciple must deny themselves and take up their cross daily and follow me," said Jesus in Luke 9:23. Sitting in the hospital room, watching nurses and techs come and go, administering aid to Greg, I thought of the sovereignty of King Jesus. Thinking of Sam's autism diagnosis, I remembered how Christ molded us through that. I thought of my previous divorce and escape from the hellish nightmare of a domestic violence-infused marriage, and how Christ protected and guided me during that time.

All the past incidents held, within their pain and hardship, lessons to be learned about the character of God. I had to slow down in the middle of the chaos and be still, to see God work in the middle of the mayhem. I had to get out of the way.

For followers of Christ, taking up our cross daily means, every single day—look for Jesus. Give that day to Him. The good, bad, mediocre, and the fantastic. Make the day fit around Jesus, not Jesus around the day. Kneeling on the hospital floor in front of that black leather bench, I would pour my heart out to Him in gratitude, thanking Him for placing the bullet, for friends who came to see us that morning, for the law enforcement officers who were working the case. Taking up our cross daily means that no matter what happens in life, we actively seek and see Jesus' sovereignty instead of focusing on our hardships.

Why does the Luke Scripture say "daily?" It's in the daily humdrum of life that we are weakest. Get up in the morning, go about our day, feed the family, baths, go to bed, get up in the morning—day in and out, it's the same thing. It is way too easy to slip into a gorge of mediocrity and stop relying on Christ when our days become one big blur.

Every single day is an opportunity to do something for the Kingdom of God—whether that is a smile, or sharing Jesus with someone, texting a friend that you thought of them, or bigger things like diving into the Word to see what the Bible says about an issue your child is facing.

Surrendering to Jesus' sovereignty means you acknowledge Him as Lord over your own life. It is committing yourself to the will of God, that no matter what happens, God knows best. He knows the plans He has for us. We do not, and we are not God.

Our friend Anne and her son Colby visited us in the hospital that morning, after the first prayer service. After she checked in with Greg, she and Colby encouraged me to come with them to the cafeteria. She bought breakfast for me and told me to eat, that I had to keep up my strength and my own health.

Christ's hands and feet, she was Jesus' messenger to me that morning, telling me that He knew what was good for me, and I was to fall into His arms for care and comfort. I seriously doubt I would have eaten breakfast that morning had it not been for Anne visiting us while the second prayer service at church was still going strong. Her obedience to the One who cooked breakfast for the disciples provided breakfast to me.

I love what Paul said to the Roman centurions and sailors at the end of Acts. There was a violent storm and the ship taking Paul and others to Rome capsized. The Bible says that Paul did the amazing act of encouraging his captors. "Just before dawn Paul urged them all to eat. 'For the last fourteen days,' he said, 'you have been in constant suspense and have gone without food—you haven't eaten anything. Now I urge you to take some food. You need it to survive. Not one of you will lose a single hair from his head.' After he said this, he took some bread and gave thanks to God in front of them all. Then he broke it and began to eat. They were all encouraged and ate some food themselves," [Acts 27:33-36 NIV]. Paul knew that in Rome, soldiers who lost a prisoner found themselves on the receiving end of Caesar's not-so-good graces. What stress they must have been under! Paul, being full of the grace of Jesus Christ, extended comfort to his captors and prepared a meal for *them.*

I love that Jesus cares enough about us to not only provide our daily bread but encourage us to eat it. We should partake of Jesus, the Bread of Life, with the same enthusiasm as eating bread. His ways are sovereign even when it comes to caring for the caregivers.

Chapter Three
A Choice To Be Made

Let the redeemed of the Lord tell their story—
those he redeemed from the hand of the foe.
Psalm 107:2

ໄ

Later that morning, going down in the elevator to
grab a soda from the cafeteria, I suddenly realized
that the news media would probably want to talk with
us. I decided right then Greg would be out of the
loop on that. He needed to focus all his energy on
himself. With a background and education in
journalism, the media would be my job.

As I got off the elevator, wondering about this and
what I would say, Jesus spoke: *you have a choice,*
Terrie. Proclaim the Gospel of forgiveness in Me.

Or don't.

Faith in Christ is a highly intentional verb. It's an
active, moving, alive faith: knowing Christ, the Son of
the Living God, brings us through tragedies not to
harm us (although Greg was paralyzed and in great

pain), but to use us to show His glory to a lost and fallen world.

That is *Kingdom Vision*. Not wallowing in despair over acts of sinful men, but remembering that we, as Christians, are being watched. Closely. We are being watched by non-Christians just to see how we mess up or get hurt--and how we handle that. Kingdom Vision is having God's Big Picture at work in our lives. Kingdom Vision is what we use to square up opportunities to share the Gospel, despite tragedies that fill our own lives.

Jesus promised us, "I have told you these things, so that in me you may have peace. In this world you will have trouble. But take heart! I have overcome the world," [John 16:33 NIV]. He didn't say we *may* have trouble, or trouble only on Tuesdays. He said we *will* have trouble in this world. But..*Jesus has overcome the world.*

We as Christians always have a choice, to either go about our lives *pretending* that all is wonderful or being *authentic* and *real.* Life is not easy. It's not supposed to be a walk in the park with wildlife creatures cleaning your house and singing. But it's in the hard things of life that we grow the most in Christ.

If it was said once, it was said a dozen times then and throughout the years since the shooting: *It's in the Bible: God won't put any more on you than you can handle.* Not only is this *not* in the Bible, it is against the character of God, and is a twisting of scripture by satan himself.

The verse those well-meaning people are trying to quote is 1 Corinthians 10:13. "No temptation has overtaken you except what is common to mankind. And God is faithful; he will not let you be tempted beyond what you can bear. But when you are tempted, he will also provide a way out so that you can endure it" [NIV]. This verse is talking about *temptation.* It says *nothing* about not putting more on us than we can handle.

Think about this: if we can handle whatever life threw at us, that would make little gods of us, wouldn't it? When we *cannot* handle whatever curveball is thrown our way, we acknowledge our desperate need for God in prayer and supplication– and *He* gets the glory. Not us. We only share in the glory that God provides in the light of Christ's atoning work on the cross. Romans 8:17 states, "Now if we are children, then we are heirs—heirs of God and co-heirs with Christ, if indeed we share in his sufferings in order that we may also share in his glory," [NIV]. We share in *suffering* so that we might display *His* glory to others.

It's all about choices. Greg told someone recently, "I have a choice to get out of bed in the morning and go to work, just like you do. I have a choice to either feel sorry for myself or not. I have a choice to be me or be this paraplegic man who was a victim. I choose not to be a victim, but an instrument of God's grace and mercy."

To God be the glory.

∾

Late Sunday morning, Greg was moved to a step-down unit from the TICU to a regular room, which was unheard-of for someone with the type of injury he had. Still on extensive pain medications and not eating, his body was reeling from shock. Because he was sleeping a lot, he did not notice all the nurses coming and going, checking vitals, cathing him, and encouraging him to drink water.

Jacob had driven Greg's truck back to the hospital. He was pale; dark circles were under his eyes: he had not slept at all. The tell-tale signs of heavy crying were all over him.

Down in the cafeteria, Jacob and I talked about the immediate future. The truck was now his to drive. He had to go back to the university, but first his license needed to be renewed and the taxes were due on the truck, which required an inspection. He was overwhelmed, dealing with raw and unforgiving emotions in addition to trying to handle a tough first semester at college. He was hurting and reeling from the events of the last 24 hours. Reaching across the table, I took his hand in mine and we took all of it to

the Lord, praying with bowed heads in the cafeteria.
The Lord would provide—He had provided so far.

❦

After noon, the hospital room flooded with church
family members, who brought snacks and magazines.
Concerned and worried, offering up prayers and
petitions on our behalf, they took turns coming in
the room and seeing us, then going to the waiting
room to pray. Many slipped money or checks into
my hand, saying that they knew how expensive it was
to stay at the hospital. A feeling of helplessness
surrounded everyone—helpless to do anything other
than pray and provide funds or food. It was enough.
It was enough.

❦

In the early afternoon, Gary and Barbara walked
uneasily into the room, unsure of what they would
find. Fighting tears and anger, they held Greg's hand
as he slept. Barbara, a nurse, examined his facial
wounds and talked with the medical staff. Gary kept
vigil beside the bed, holding his son's hand. It was

obvious he was struggling between incredible grief and worry, and intense anger.

Jacob visited with the people in the waiting room while, at the urging of Gary and Barbara, I went to the cafeteria with them. As we ate dinner, across the tables, I saw a man with long dreads out of the corner of my eye, and my breath caught in my throat. My heart raced, my palms sweated—Barbara looked in the direction I was staring and reached across for my hand. The man turned; it wasn't one of the shooters—just a man with dreadlocks visiting a friend or family member in the hospital.

I couldn't believe my reaction at the man in the cafeteria. The immediate sense of panic and fear, the intimidating desire to run up and clock him—all of it took me totally by surprise. Nausea welled up inside me, shocked and ashamed at my thoughts in that moment. This is not me, I thought, this is not me. Sweating and heart racing, I suddenly became aware that Gary was gently encouraging me to go home, to rest. Barbara nodded, still holding my hand. That was such a foreign concept to me, going home when my husband laid in a hospital bed from a gunshot wound.

"Terrie," Gary said, "We are worried about Greg, but he is in good hands. We are more worried about you at this point. You need rest. We'll stay with Greg tonight—go home and rest, come back in the morning."

With Gary and Barbara staying at the hospital, I felt better about leaving. While Jacob drove the truck home, I drove the SUV, still loaded with suitcases from Thanksgiving. I called my mom, gave her an update, and spoke with Laura. She was scared and worried; trying to reassure her was a hard hill to climb.

We had been in the house less than five minutes when the doorbell rang. Jacob, immediately on guard, answered it. A reporter from a local TV station wanted to interview me. I told him that I was exhausted, and needed to change my shirt, but if he could promise it would be less than ten minutes it would be okay. He agreed, leaving me to change my shirt and brush my hair while he retrieved the camera.

In the interview, I gave a brief summary of what happened and how Greg was doing. The reporter asked if I had anything to say to the men who did this horrific act. Suddenly, I said that I forgive them.

The reporter did a double-take. "What? You...forgive them?"

"Yes," I said. "As Christ has forgiven us, so we forgive them."

The choice had been made. In this, Christ would be glorified.

Chapter Four
Why Do Bad Things Happen to Good People?

"By the sweat of your brow you will eat your food until you return to the ground, since from it you were taken; for dust you are and to dust you will return."
Psalm 107:2

❧

The question is not, *Why us?* The question is, *Why not us?* Why do bad things happen to good people?

The short answer is this: *sin.*

When Eve made the choice to listen to satan instead of God in the Garden of Eden, she not only brought damnation upon herself and her husband, *who was standing right there and did not stop her,* but also all their descendants and even Creation itself. God told Adam:

"Because you listened to your wife and ate fruit from the tree about which I commanded you, 'You must not eat from it,' cursed is the ground because of you; through painful toil you will eat food from it all the days of your life. It will produce thorns and thistles for you, and you will eat the plants of the field. By the sweat of your brow you will eat your food until you return to the ground, since from it you were taken; for dust you are and to dust you will return," [Genesis 3:17-19 NIV].

Before sin appeared on the Earth, there were no weeds, briars, or thorns. Sin brought these dastardly hurtful things on the planet. No longer would the Lord God walk with his children in the cool of the Garden, talking and in perfect fellowship. Committing that first sin was as much a choice as Darren had when he pulled the trigger.

Because of Darren and Terrell's choice, Greg is paralyzed. Another way: Because of Darren's sin, Greg is paralyzed. All sins affect others—even the ones done in shadow and mystery. Just as Adam and Eve's sin affected all of humanity, Darren and Terrell's sin affected us, causing Greg to be paralyzed. All of us experienced ramifications of that terrible night.

Now, some might ask, where was God? Don't we often hear that from nonbelievers during times of trauma and tragedy? Asking that question shows not only a lack of faith but also a lack of knowledge about the character of God.

God placed the bullet square in the L1 vertebrae, making Greg paralyzed but not killing him. He allowed or even led that man to spit in the water fountain, causing the custodian to clean it with bleach water, which gave a perfect canvas upon which Terrell left two perfect latent fingerprints.

Where was God? Scripture says that He "hem(s) me in behind and before, and you lay your hand upon me," [Psalm 139:5 NIV]. As we were shuffling boxes around the morning of November 28, God was already moving. As we were waving goodbye, God was putting into place the detectives, the troopers, even the custodian–setting the stage with all the players He wanted in this drama. He went before us and came up behind us.

As I was driving down I-85 to the hospital, seeing a sea of red lights ahead of me, it was Jesus who heard my heartfelt and desperate prayers to "split the Red Sea again." With my hazard lights blinking and horn blaring, Jesus moved the cars in front of me and allowed me to drive right down the middle line between the cars. It's all Jesus. He is sovereign.

Sovereignty means God rules all. We may think we have it all figured out, and we're in charge, but we aren't in charge of anything. We shake our fists heavenward and say, "When I get to heaven, I will ask God _____."

I love what God said to Job. "Then the LORD spoke to Job out of the storm. He said: "Who is this that obscures my plans with words without knowledge? Brace yourself like a man; I will question you, and you shall answer me" [Job 38:1-3].

It did no good to demand an answer for the shooting from God. Did God allow it? No, and yes. While Greg getting shot was the natural consequence of sin, God has bigger plans for Greg and everyone affected *through* the shooting.

Luke 8:2 states that Jesus cast seven demons out of Mary Magdalene. Why had seven demons possessed her? We have no idea why seven demons took control of her mind, when one would have done the trick. What horror she had to have experienced! What possible good could have come out of demon possession seven-fold?

When Jesus cast them out, Mary Magdalene, in her right mind and freed of the torment she had suffered, became a staunch supporter and disciple of her Lord. In fact, the five times in Scripture she is not named within a group of other female disciples, she is a leading lady in the story of Christ's death and resurrection. In fact, it is Mary Magdalene who, after experiencing the risen Savior, runs to tell the other disciples that the tomb was empty. Glory!

As seven in biblical terms means "completeness," perhaps Mary was possessed by so many demons to illustrate that she was completely overwrought with sin and wickedness. With Christ's healing, the seven demons drive home the point that only Jesus could completely and permanently heal her. No one else. Only a complete healing from the One Savior could completely eradicate wickedness. After the change of management, she had a purpose and mission drastically different than her life before: to share her Savior with others.

Greg was shot in a senseless crime, but Jesus has a higher purpose than for Greg to be a statistic. Before the shooting, he was wrestling with depression and weight gain. He didn't have an understanding of what the Lord had in store for him. But God did.

The Bible says, "'For I know the plans I have for you,' declares the LORD, 'plans to prosper you and not to harm you, plans to give you hope and a future. Then you will call on me and come and pray to me, and I will listen to you'" (Jeremiah 29:11-12 NIV). Verse 11 is often quoted but verse 12 is just as powerful. When bad things happen, we need to look at them as plans that the Lord has put in our path, not to harm us, but to draw us closer to Him. When we call on Him, He is faithful and just, and will listen to us.

This is a hard concept, especially for people who have had loved ones die in shootings, bombings, terrorist activities, and car accidents. This is a hard concept for parents who are holding lifeless little ones, or children who have been hurt. As followers of Christ, we must have the faith that our Lord is Lord in the good times *and* in the bad.

Some people might ask, why didn't God stop the shooting? *Greg is alive, isn't he?* Had that bullet traveled one-half of an inch in any direction, he would not be here today. The bullet was fired from less than three feet away—the detective called it a "kill shot." But God is sovereign. He did not want Greg dead. He wanted to use Greg *because of the shooting* to minister to others.

This is a hard thing to understand, but just perhaps, we are not meant to understand it. Some things are too hard for us to grasp, and we cannot imagine a sovereign God who would allow such wickedness. Listen: when sin entered the world, everything changed. Ramifications of sin meant that all would pay the consequences. This is little hope in the unnatural act of a parent burying a child, but just as much as we cry, Jesus cries too.

Jesus cries because He knows what started all this mess in the first place: rebellion against His sovereignty in the Garden of Eden. He cries when His children—you and I—experience the ramifications of sins like murder, bullying, pornography addictions, and drunkenness.

Jacob, when he was little, rebelled right after his dad and I divorced. He started shoplifting. After discovering a little stuffed bear in his room that I didn't recognize, I questioned him about it. The truth came out: he shoplifted the bear from a restaurant that had a gift shop. He and I drove to the restaurant, where I asked for the manager and made Jacob tell what he had done. I then made Jacob pay for the bear, and we walked out with it. He was told that despite money eventually being exchanged for the bear, he could not have it. I had him throw it in a trashcan at the restaurant. Jacob's sin of stealing meant the bear went into the trash and he lost a stuffed animal. There were ramifications that occurred.

Where was God the night of the shooting? Jesus prevented Greg from passing out as he looked inches away into a pool of his own blood, enabling him to give the trooper detailed descriptions of the suspects. He delivered strength to me to keep Jacob from going after those men, who would have hurt or killed him. He provided someone to comfort Laura when I had to be helping Greg and talking with police. Jesus was there in every God-ordered step. No, Jesus did not *prevent* the shooting, but He did something even more powerful: He demonstrated His incredible grace to us.

Grace is giving a gift to someone who doesn't deserve it. We did not deserve Jesus' power, presence, and peace that night, but He gave it to us anyway, knowing that we needed it. Because of that grace shown to us, we must extend that same grace to other undeserving people, namely, Darren, Terrell, and Keyona.

Greg dealt (and is dealing) with the ramifications of Darren and Terrell's sin of shooting him, however— in God's sovereignty, this was part of a bigger plan that He had for us all. We had to go through the desert to get to the promised land—and we had to trust Jesus that the promised land was on the other side of the desert though we could not see it over the towering mountains that lay before us.

Romans 8:28 (NIV) states: "And we know that in all things God works for the good of those who love him, who have been called according to his purpose."

This passage can be an extraordinarily hard one to understand, given the pain that life can bring. We don't want to think of our God as being Someone who orchestrates hardship upon our lives. That's not what this powerful verse is sharing. "We know that *in all things*." Even in life's deepest hurts, even when it involves someone being paralyzed or killed, *in all things*, God is moving. He is in the background and the foreground, working things out *for the good of those who love Him.*

This may mean that He works in us and gives us a choice: to retreat in our misery and become bitter, which hurts our health more; or to reach out for

Him, extend forgiveness, and move forward with our lives—whatever that entails.

Chapter Five
Sadness of Heart

...Why does your face look so sad when you are not
ill? This can be nothing but sadness of heart....
Nehemiah 2:2a

❧

Barbara had innocently posted a small snippet about
the shooting on social media, before I had had a
chance to do so. She had wanted to mobilize the
armies of prayer warriors, and mobilize they did.
Prayers were pouring in from all over the world.

In our shock, we had made a critical mistake: reeling
from the trauma, we neglected to call Greg's
daughter Elli, at her mother's house in Pennsylvania,
about her daddy. She had been sitting on the sofa,
going through social media, when she happened
upon her Grandma's post. Stunned, she read it over
and over, then let out a screaming cry.

Her step-sister and mother tried to comfort her, but
to no avail. She *needed* to see her daddy, to know
for herself he was alive.

It was decided: she was in no shape to drive herself, so her mother called Barbara for the hospital information. She and Elli would be driving down as soon as possible.

∾

Jacob called Sam, and he talked with him at length about the shooting. He reassured Sam that Greg was okay. Injured and paralyzed, but alive.

Sam did not understand "paralyzed." Jacob told him that Greg's legs no longer worked. He could not walk, or stand, or run.

"Okay," said Sam, with a marked change in his voice. "I will learn how to build robot legs for him. Out of my toy bricks. Will you tell him that?"

Jacob choked back tears. "Yes, Sam. I will tell him."

Chapter Six
The Day is Almost Here

The night is nearly over; the day is almost here. So let us put aside the deeds of darkness and put on the armor of light.
Romans 13:12

و

After the reporter left the house, Jacob and I settled down for the night: laundry was going, he was packing to leave for college, and I took a much-needed long, hot shower. I cried myself to sleep that night on Greg's side of the bed, using his pillow that smelled like him. Oh how I missed my husband.

The next morning, I took a duffle bag of Laura's clothes to my Mom's apartment. When Laura saw me, she immediately burst into tears and grabbed me. I picked her up and held her tight. Sitting on the sofa, Mom and I talked about the shooting and the time afterward; with Laura on my lap, Mom wrapped her arms around me as I cried.

I took Mom and Laura for a quick trip to the grocery, and we went by our church. Leaving Mom in the car, Laura and I went in. She had been saving coins for the China Mission Trip, and she wanted to bring them to the office as that day was the deadline. Tears brimmed in the eyes of the ladies in the church office as Laura handed over her mason jar. Down the hall, Pastor Ronnie called me to his office. Chris, Pastor Jeff, and Pastoral Counselor Larry sat with him at a small round table; they pulled a chair up for me.

They said they had been talking amongst themselves about how to help us. They said that they knew our home needed to be renovated for a wheelchair, and they wanted to take that on. Jeff would work on a crowdfunding campaign; Chris would coordinate the construction logistics. Larry asked how they could help us emotionally and spiritually. Overwhelmed with gratitude, I just sat and cried and thanked them. I told Larry that prayers were coveted. Chris said that I needed to get whatever I thought we needed out of the house. Ronnie asked if I had a place to live while the house was being renovated; I said, "My mom's. It would be the best since she's keeping Laura."

Ronnie asked about meals. I said that my mom could use meals for her and Laura, just to take that weight off her.

God showed up. By the time I was getting to the car with Laura, I was weeping; Mom asked me what in the world was wrong? I told her: "God is going to reno the house through the church!" Her mouth flew open; she had never experienced such grace.

Still astounded, I dropped Mom and Laura off at the apartment, and went back home to get Jacob, who had finished his laundry and was packed for school. Leaving his luggage, we drove the thirty minutes back to the hospital, talking about ways to get the truck inspected, his license updated, and other necessary but time-intensive errands.

Greg was awake and attempting to eat a little breakfast as he visited with his parents. Chris was there, having left the church right after the meeting and beating us to the hospital.

Greg mentioned the truck, and that Jacob was going to drive it now, but things had to be done for that to happen. He looked at me and commented that Jacob and I needed to go back to Gastonia and get all that done.

"No," Chris said. "Jacob and I will get that done. No problem." He left with Jacob—God answered another major prayer right in front of us.

Tears were actively seeping out of eyes: Barbara's, Gary's, and my own as I relayed the church meeting to them. Greg was in intense pain and not trying to hide it, but could talk, eat a little, and drink water from a Styrofoam pitcher and cup. Visitors had come in before Jacob and I; a wooden crate filled with snacks, magazines, word search books, and fresh fruit sat on the windowsill. Every few minutes a new visitor came in, apprehensively at first, but they quickly relaxed when they saw Greg. Despite pain, the calmness and peace that was over him was from Christ alone; guests, nurses, and doctors all commented on it.

The next morning, as I was at the hospital, Jacob left for school. He and Chris had had the truck inspected, registration paid, and license updated. It was incredibly hard, this time around, to have him leave. I knew he had not dealt with the shooting and was about to finish a hard semester with intense uncertainty. Yet, there he went—covered in prayers.

There were so many people visiting us at the hospital that the nursing staff moved Greg across the hall, to a larger room. This room had a rudimentary sofa, only a tad more comfortable than the recliner, but at least visitors had a place on which to sit.

We were just in a holding pattern—trying to get pain managed and deal with an unknown future. We interacted with visitors; I would go out of the hospital and walk across the street to talk with reporters, as they weren't allowed on hospital property. Friends shared my posts and news reports on social media.

I had made the decision to hold off on blogging on my website, NearYourAltar.com, for a while. I could only do so much; that was one thing that had to go to the back burner for a season. Two months before, I had self-published my first book, an Advent devotional, and while I had had plans to market it for the Christmas season, that was also off the radar.

Fellow bloggers, whom I had met at a conference in October and online, knew of the shooting. They took my book's social media presence and ran with it, encouraging people to buy it to help provide funds for us. They shared posts off my website to keep traffic up. Jesus, who cared about my little Christian encouragement blog, worked through my writing friends to make the site have the most traffic it had had since it was started. I was in awe of the goodness of God—that He would do this for my family and me. I felt so very unworthy and humbled that, while He was working on Greg's injuries and other people in that hospital, He was also working to keep traffic up on my site.

Greg's past depression seemed to have been obliterated. I remembered, the past summer, praying that Jesus would heal him of depression...never in my wildest dreams would I think being shot and paralyzed would shatter the dark cloud of depression that had hung over Greg. He talked of the peace that Christ was laying on him and His tangible presence. Though he could not feel his legs, his soul was soaring with Christ.

Our family doctor called me. While I paced in the hallway, she told me she had been watching the news with her husband when the report about the shooting appeared. She told me, "I popped my husband on the arm and yelled, 'That's my family!' I cannot believe what happened! Tell me: what do you need?"

My doctor and I had (and still have) the kind of relationship that, if she weren't my doctor, we could be best friends. I told her that I needed something to calm my nerves and something to help me sleep. She replied, "Done. Pick it up at the office tomorrow. Now—tell me about Greg."

I gave her a medical run-down. She listened intently. She wanted to know how Jacob was doing, and especially Laura, who she calls her "little surgeon-general" due to Laura's interest in being a doctor, nurse, or paleontologist (it changes often). We hung up; she had encouraged me more than anyone. Walking back to the room, Barbara met me in the hallway; I told her about the call. She began to weep—the kindnesses being shown to her family were almost too much to bear.

Early in the morning of December 2, while it was still dark, three hours away in the observation booth at a state prison, a guard was working the graveyard shift. As the video feed from several prison cameras feed into the booth's many monitors, a television in the room was tuned to a local news station. The guard sipped coffee and watched the monitors.

The news anchor on the television behind him said in a dramatic, non-accented voice, "The father of four special needs children who was gunned down at a rest area on I-85 is paralyzed..."

Interest piqued, the guard slowly spun around to the television, keeping his attention on the monitors until the last second. He brought the cup up and sipped hot coffee at the exact moment the news showed the footage of Darren's powerful stride before the drink machines in the vending area. Coffee spewed out of his mouth; the guard uttered a curse word and grabbed the radio. He had recognized Darren and his power walk from when he was a prisoner, not six weeks prior.

Minutes later, his supervisor joined him in the booth. Both watched the video on the news' social media page. They played it several times, and they both confirmed Darren's identity. "Call the Cabarrus county sheriff's department," the supervisor told the guard. "We know who that is and where he lives."

In the days since the shooting, Darren had disposed of the gun and his cell phone; he cut his dreads, stuffing them in a brown paper bag along with the clothes he had worn that night. He placed the bag where he thought police would not look: in his mother's car. Using a burner phone, he had texted and called Terrell repeatedly. He called Keyona, although she was done with him. Thinking it was best he lay low, he hunkered down in his mother's house and played video games.

His mother was home on December 3 as Darren was playing video games. Someone knocked on the door and Darren's mother answered it; suddenly the house was swarmed with police and S.W.A.T officers, screaming "Get down! Hands in the air!"

Darren, in handcuffs, found himself being questioned by the same detective that had visited the hospital the night of the shooting.

He was shrugging everything off during questioning when the police turned to his mother. Irate with her son, she went outside with a detective and produced the brown paper bag of clothing and hair from her car.

Suddenly, Darren was singing a different tune. Sighing, he asked the lead detective for paper and pen: it was time he confessed; he wrote his statement on the yellow legal pad before he was handcuffed and placed in a squad car. He was taken to the Cabarrus County detention center.

∾

Life began to take on a new normal. Elli and her mother, then Gary and Barbara, left to go to their respective homes. Greg insisted that I go home and come in the next day with Laura. She was scared and crying a lot, and needed to see that her daddy, while injured severely, was still alive.

I drove home, and a song came on the radio: "Same Power" by Jeremy Camp[1]. I sung it at the very top of my lungs, claiming each line of lyrics for victory in Jesus, tears carving lines down my cheeks. I knew, right in that moment, that this was going to be a new normal, and just as Jesus had been with us in the new

---

[1] ["Same Power," *I Will Follow* by Jeremy Camp. Stolen Pride Records in association with Sparrow Records and Capitol Christian Music Group, February 3, 2015].

normals of Sam's autism, being a single mom, then a blended family, it was going to be okay. Jesus showed me in that moment that a man could use a weapon and injure my husband, but he could not take away Jesus' love for Greg or our children, or me.

On the way home, Jesus spoke to me through each song played on my local Christian radio station, WMIT 106.9 The Light. It was as if Jesus was the DJ for the late afternoon drive home. Song after song ministered to me; by the time I turned in the driveway I was expecting to either hold a revival or be raptured.

At home by myself, I showered, packed bags, and loaded an air mattress and air pump in the car. I was reading and highlighting passages in my Bible, late that night, when Greg called.

"They got him," he said.

I gasped. "They did?"

"They have a two-million-dollar bond on him."

Another gasp. "No! Really?" I said, astonished.

"Yeah," Greg said. "No bondsman will touch that."

"How are you?" I asked, hearing some discomfort in Greg's voice.

"Oh, you know, paralyzed. In a lot of pain. The nurses this shift aren't on top of pain management like last shift."

Greg's sense of humor made me shake my head. "Do I need to come up?"

"No," he said, abruptly. "No need for us both to not sleep. Are you bringing Laura up tomorrow?"

"Yes, and tomorrow night I'll be staying with Mom."

"Okay baby. I love you," Greg said, his voice cracking in pain.

"I love you," I said, and ended the call. I hopped on social media, pulled up my account, wrote "THEY GOT HIM," hit "post."

My head hit the pillow, sighing, "Lord Jesus, thank you. Thank you." Sleep came quickly and deeply on Greg's side of the bed.

Chapter Seven
The Lord Builds the House

*Unless the Lord builds the house, the builders labor
in vain. Unless the Lord watches over the city,
the guards stand watch in vain.*
Psalm 127:1

Immediately after learning that Darren had been
arrested, Terrell and his wife drove overnight to the
New York City area. Staying one night at his family's
house, and another night at her family's house, they
moved from couch to sofa throughout the area. An
acquaintance asked Terrell to drive him to the
grocery store and back to his house in Queens.

The Federal Bureau of Investigation, working in
cooperation with the Cabarrus County Crime
Investigation Unit, followed Terrell's cell phone
pings on towers from North Carolina throughout the
New York City metro area. Suddenly, Terrell started
talking to his acquaintance as they were driving
around Queens about this "old guy" he and Darren
had popped, and that another friend of

Terrell's was blowing his phone up about the borrowed gun that had been used in the attempted armed robbery. In this conversation, Terrell told his friend all about the shooting, his role in it, and that he had shot another man a few hours before, in Hillsborough. Right before this conversation started, somehow, someway, an app on his phone that he had used to record rap songs mysteriously turned on—and the listening ears at the FBI recorded the entire conversation.

Terrell had no idea.

Laura and I woke up the next morning, showered and dressed, and grabbed breakfast on the way to the hospital. She asked questions about her daddy: "Is he alive? Can he walk? Is he bleeding?"

She was preparing herself.

I calmed her as best I could with information that her five-year-old precocious self could handle.

"Daddy cannot walk. He is in a lot of pain. You can hug Daddy, but you can't get on him..."

I sighed: no mother should have to say these things, I thought. "Daddy has a lot of wires and tubes attached to him. He has an IV—like you had when you were in the hospital for your migraines, remember? And they're giving him shots in his IV. But he's the same Daddy."

"Okay, Mommy," Laura said, looking out the window. "And the bad men won't be there?"

"No," I said, biting my lip to keep from crying. "The bad men won't be there."

Laura held my hand on the elevator, after pushing the button for Greg's floor. She looked up at me and said, "I'm scared."

Putting my hand on her shoulder, I said, "It's okay to be scared."

Sighing, she held my hand tightly as we stepped off the elevator and walked in silence down the hall to Greg's room.

She stopped at the door; Greg saw her and called out one of her nicknames: "Puffie-poo!"

She burst into tears; here was her daddy! In a hospital gown and with a really bad cut on his nose, but he was the same daddy!

He held out his arms on the side of the bed and she ran to him in the first hug she had from him since before the shooting. He hugged her tight as she bawled into his hospital gown. "Here," he said, "Get up here."

"No, Greg, it's okay," I said.

"No," he said, chin quivering. "It's okay." He put his hands beside him and, groaning, face contorted, lifted himself bit-by-bit until he had scooted over enough for Laura to lie down beside him. I picked her up and put her in the spot Greg had made for her. She wiggled herself into his armpit area, throwing an arm over his chest. She sighed with contentment and happiness.

"She needed this," he said, holding her.

"I think you needed it too," I said, eking out a smile for the first time in days.

"Yeah," Greg said, kissing the top of her head. "God is so good."

The next day, I left Mom's apartment and drove to the house. My friend Shiela came with her children, and immediately got to work on helping me pack up the master bedroom closets, taking the clothes to my car. A group of friends from church was going to be at the house later, to start demo.

All the media attention and social shares garnered an overnight blessing of funds in the crowdfunding site. Total strangers were giving of their financial resources to help the paralyzed man with four special needs kids. God the Provider was pouring His provision upon us in a mighty way.

Shiela was in the kitchen, directing her kids, while I was digging shoes out of the bottom of Greg's closet. I reached way back, and pulled out his well-worn, black-and-white golf shoes with ground-in plastic spikes that had seen years of use.

The shoes that would never see a green or fairway again.

I gripped those shoes and bellowed; heaving sobs racked my chest. Shiela ran to the bedroom, dropped to her knees and grabbed me. She held me, there on the closet floor, and let days' worth of sobs pour out as I held the shoes tight to my chest. "There, there," she said. "Let it out, it's okay..."

"It just...hit me," I said, fighting trying to talk, breathe, and sob all at once. "He won't...be able to...play golf again."

Her tears were sprinkling upon my head as she held me tight. "I can't imagine what you're feeling," she whispered.

"No one can," I said, sitting up and wiping my eyes on the sleeve of my hoodie.

Shiela stood up, stretched her back. "They will be here soon, but take your time. I know this has to be hard."

We picked up more things in the closet, taking them to my car. The closet and bathroom were spaces of contention with me. It was a walk-through closet, with a tiny closet on either side of an equally tiny hallway, leading to a small three-piece master bath. A toilet, one sink, and a tub made up the bathroom, with very minimal storage. Greg had built the wooden over-the-toilet shelf unit, and that was it for storage. We had plans to remodel the bathroom, kitchen, and living room but we never had the money or the time.

A friendly voice greeted us from the living room. Chris walked in, a bundle of energy, followed by more people who immediately started moving furniture to a storage unit that had been delivered to our driveway the night before, along with a long construction dumpster. As soon as living room furniture was out, carpet began to be ripped up and thrown in the dumpster. Another crew started demolishing the master bathroom.

The same reporter that had visited the first night home arrived to film the latest story in the saga that was our lives: "Gastonia church remodels home of rest stop shooting victim." He asked if I could speak with him, so I did, again, this time in the front yard. More reporters showed up, from our local newspaper and another television station.

Repeating the same things over and over—how Greg was doing, how we felt about the house remodel—began to wear on me, sitting on the porch swing. I was in the middle of giving an interview, on camera, whilst a newspaper photographer was taking pictures of me. I repeated that we had forgiven the shooters, that it's a daily process, and it's just really hard to believe this was our reality now.

The reporters started asking Chris questions. Hands shaking, tears falling, stomach in knots, I felt like the entire world was spinning. I felt out of control of myself, dizzy and faint. I went inside and told Shiela, "Look, I have to get out of here."

"Go," she said. "You need to be anywhere but here right now."

My friend Amy hugged me tight, told me to go get lunch, then go to Greg. I couldn't eat lunch. There was no way. Nausea was overcoming me. I walked out the back door, to the workshop, and closed the shop door behind me.

Greg's woodworking tools sat, quiet, in the darkness. As filtered light shone from around the door, I sat on a pile of lumber and looked at all his unfinished projects. Another crying jag took control of my body with shaking heaves; I struggled to get my breath. It was all so unreal, what was happening in the chill of an early December day. We were *supposed* to have had our Christmas tree up; he was *supposed* to have been at work; I was *supposed* to have been inside at the dining room table, homeschooling Laura. We should have been practicing counting to 20 that day instead of having our house gutted to match our hearts.

We were so very appreciative of what our church family was doing; but in that appreciation was a large swath of sorrow. It's not that we weren't grateful, it was the circumstances—the *why*—behind the house being demolished and renovated that was just too much to take.

"Lord Jesus," I whispered through a cloud of tears staining my face and falling on sawdust. "You are blessing us just as you blessed David when you built his house. It's a different type of house, but like David, we are so unworthy. Thank you for Your grace. Thank you for the house You are building us through Your people, the church. Amen."

Sitting there in the darkness, the cross of Christ came to mind. Christ sacrificed Himself on the cross, had to go through dying, to bear the sins of the world. He surrendered all on the cross to raise to life three days later. The renovation that was the Resurrection could not happen without the demolition that was the cross.

My knees hit the sawdust, my hands outstretched. "Thank you, Jesus, thank you for the cross. We could not celebrate an empty tomb without You on the cross. Thank you."

Chapter Eight
Whatever Situation

Nevertheless, each person should live as a believer in whatever situation the Lord has assigned to them, just as God has called them....
1 Corinthians 7:17a

The hard part of a "new normal" while still dealing with the non-normality of a hospital stay is you lose all sense of reality. While Greg was in the hospital, then moved next door to rehab, the house was still undergoing renovations while Laura and I stayed at Mom's. Mom tried to continue homeschooling Laura as best as she could, but Laura's fragile spirit made lessons difficult. While she took care of Laura, I made the 45-minute drive to the hospital every morning to be there for Greg.

Due to the suspects' gang involvement, the police worked with the hospital in making sure Greg was safe. Part of this required an alias on his part, because of all the media attention with his real name. He decided his new first name would be his real

middle name—Donald— and he thought of our friend
Kammie's oldest daughter, Taylor, who had come
with her mother and sister Morgan to the hospital
the night of the shooting. We consider both girls to
be Christ-nieces; not related biologically or by
marriage, but something more powerful: the Blood
of Jesus. So Greg became "Donald Taylor" in rehab.

I still called him Greg.

His rehab quickly became *our* rehab, as we both
learned how to navigate this new normal. Greg
worked diligently and deliberately at learning new
ways of body management in occupational and
physical therapies. While he learned how to shower,
I learned how to help him transfer from a wheelchair
to a shower chair. When he learned how to dress, I
intentionally paid close attention to his needs, even
though he may not have known what they were at the
time.

Armed with information gleaned from watching him,
I would stop at a discount store and pick up diabetic
socks to prevent circulation issues and elastic-waist

knit pajama pants for ease of dressing and undressing. When I brought the bags of clothes to him, he was amazed: he didn't know what he didn't know.

That became somewhat of a theme. While a binder on spinal cord injuries was given to us, it left out information that, ultimately, we had to figure out on our own. This was an integral part of rehab: figuring out what worked and what didn't, and sometimes that changed depending on the day and the side of the bed from which Greg wanted to transfer. Until we were thrown into this world, not of our own accord, we had no idea that transfer boards, shower chairs, or bowel programs were things.

Spinal cord injuries at the L1 vertebrae affect one's ability to sense when it's time to go to the bathroom. Greg had to use a catheter to urinate: wearing disposable gloves, we both had to learn how to properly clean his penis and insert sterile, one-time-use, flexible plastic tubing into his urethra and up into his bladder. The urine would then pour out into a plastic urinal bottle. Everything had to be done with the utmost attention to cleanliness, to prevent infections.

The education continued in rehab regarding his personal care. Just like with voiding his bladder, he could no longer empty his bowels by simply sensing it was time to go, sitting on the toilet, going, and wiping. Learning the process, in rehab, of a successful bowel program was almost as traumatic as anything up to that point.

It never failed to shock me that here was a man, who, two weeks prior, was sitting on a toilet in a rest area stall, having a normal bowel movement, when he heard the voices of two guys saying they were tired of driving and had to get some money, somehow.

There is nothing dignifying about bowel programs. In rehab, Greg learned how to transfer to a raised toilet seat from the wheelchair. He had to don a hygienic disposable glove, squirt lubricant on his finger, and insert it into his rectum. Twirling his finger around on the walls of the rectum stimulated the muscles to move the feces down and out. He would start this process and end it an hour later, every night at the same time. By the time bowel program ended, he was tired and ready for bed.

It was not his favorite time of the day.

There was one night in rehab in which Greg was not feeling well. He had had a tough day in physical therapy, and then a shower after dinner. Shower nights were exhausting exercises in occupational therapy.

The nurse's assistant walked in his room to start the bowel program, just to find him in bed, nearly asleep. Elijah looked at me, then to Greg, and back at me. "You're his wife?"

"Yes," I said.

"Well," Elijah said. "Let's train you to do the bowel program when he's in bed. It's not a matter of 'if,' it's a matter of 'when.'"

Wearing blue gloves, I followed Elijah's instructions to roll Greg over to his right side, move his knees up a little, and put a clean plastic and gauze pad under his bottom. Tearing a corner off a packet of lubrication, Elijah showed me how to squirt a little on my index finger and insert the finger into Greg's rectum.

It was loose with absolutely no muscle tone.

I gagged and bit my lip.

Elijah, sensing an impending panic attack, asked gently and quietly, "Do you feel any feces?"

"Yes," I whispered.

"Pull it out with your fingers."

I scraped the feces out and it plopped onto the gauze. "Good," replied Elijah. "Now insert the same finger, and go around the inside of the rectum, touching the walls. Do that...oh, five times."

One. Two. Three. Tears. Four. Tears. Five.

"Okay," I said, sniffling.

Elijah said, "Now pull your finger out, and wait a couple of minutes. You have to let the rectum do what rectums do."

I looked at him. "When does this become normal?"

Elijah looked at me, biting his lip, eyebrows arched. "I pray it never does."

A couple quiet moments passed as I realized Greg was asleep, a little whiffling snore coming from his mouth. Elijah said, "Okay. Right. Insert that same finger and pull any feces out."

I did it. Again, it plopped onto the gauze.

"Now, take a wipe," he handed it to my clean gloved hand. "And wipe him off, front to back. Take the plastic drape to the toilet and dispose of the feces and remove your gloves. You want to take off the dirty one first, outside in, then put it on the palm of the clean glove and take it off with the dirty one inside it."

I did as he said, and he deemed it was okay. He got a call on his cell phone and had to go to another patient, leaving me to tuck Greg in. I gently rolled him on his back, slipped his CPAP mask on him, placed pillows beside his legs to keep his feet from flopping over, and covered him up. I kissed him goodnight, turned off the light, and walked out to the parking deck.

I cried all the way to Mom's apartment.

Darren, incarcerated in the Cabarrus County's jail, requested a telephone call to his girlfriend, Keyona. It was granted, but as is the case with all jailhouse communications, it was recorded.

"Keyona," Darren said, "Get hold of Terrell. Tell him, 'the old guy has to go.' I don't care how or when—he just has to go."

Keyona sighed, said, "Okay, hold on," and put Darren on hold. Using her cell phone's three-way calling feature, she tried to pull Terrell into the conversation, but the jail's communication system ended the call. Three-way calls were not allowed.

She sighed again and thought about the message. *He wants to kill that man,* she thought. She shook her head; she wanted to be done with Darren.

Trauma is not just the initial incident, such as the shooting. Trauma can also be in small, daily amounts, which add up quickly, until they create a perfect storm of emotional and psychological baggage that explodes. Here was Greg, a 6' 1" strong, heavy-built man, who played baseball in high school and coached t-ball and basketball in our church league, who enjoyed woodworking and gardening— smiling as he learned how to slide across a slick, white oak transfer board from his bed to a wheelchair. Just a few months prior, he had built a complicated closet system for a friend using wood very similar to that he was sliding upon.

He was so proud of his progress; I was nauseous with grief of what he used to be like and what those two guys took from him.

That is the most stressful thing of all in traumatic incidents that immediately change someone: the loved ones at bedside remember what the person was like before and see what the person is like afterwards. There is nothing that can be done except swallow grief and show support, then go to the bathroom and cry it out.

With Greg, it did not help at all that one of the pain medications he was on altered his personality. Usually quiet, even at home, and not much of a dramatic linguist, the pain medication made him into a showman—a loud, yappy, bubbly showman who enjoyed talking, a lot, and telling me in machine-gun fashion what to do to help him, how to do the tasks, and be quick about it.

Our LifeStudy (or Sunday School) adult class came to visit us in rehab as part of the Christmas party. In they filed, one at a time, the large group wrapping around the foot of the hospital bed and stacking up in rows so all could get in the room. Still, several people were out in the hallway where they could hear. I was between the bed and the wall on the opposite side of the room from where the door was.

Greg began to tell the story of the shooting in hugely dramatic fashion. John, his best friend and Becky's husband, had come before everyone had arrived, and was standing at the head of the bed opposite me. The more Greg delivered what can only be described as an award-winning monologue, the more he kept moving his sheets down, and he was absolutely naked under the covers.

John would reach over and pull the sheets up. Greg, still talking, pulled them down. Temperatures were messing with him and he was trying to adjust, but the pain medication messed with him. John and Greg moved together in this elaborate dance, with Greg moving the sheets down and John moving them up, with Greg's buoyant voice providing the music.

Someone asked, "Why did you stop at the rest area so close to home?"

Greg immediately zipped: "Because *she...*" and jerked a thumb my way, "...just *had* to pee!"

Gasps from around the room as I hung my head and tears fell freely.

I wanted *out*—out of that room, out of the hospital, out of the situation we had found ourselves in. Had I been able to get to the door, I would have been gone before John could pull the covers up.

Eventually, Greg's rambling gave way to more of the story even though I heard none of it. I was trying to self-calm and shake it off: *this is not my husband. This is some dude on heavy pain meds with a sick sense of humor.*

The crowd started to dissipate, and I was able to go out in the hallway. I was surrounded by loved ones offering hugs and support; every hug was a hug from Jesus from which I drew love and understanding. I explained about the medication; they all knew something wasn't right. This man playing with his covers wasn't the Greg they knew and loved and didn't want to punch.

The next morning, I walked in Greg's room to find him finishing getting dressed. He said, "Hey Lovey! I need socks; they're in that drawer. I need a t-shirt and I've got to get my hair cut. Did you get my socks yet? Where's my t-shirt?"

I had not had a chance to put my purse down when he barked orders at me; I opened a drawer. "No, Terrie," he said. "Socks are in the other drawer."

My hands were shaking. Palms sweating. I couldn't think or see. A sudden headache thundered in my brain. "I need a t-shirt!" he said with feeling: not quite yelling, but not talking with his inside voice, either.

It broke me. Throwing a pair of socks at him, then a t-shirt, heart racing, I screamed, "I CANNOT DO THIS!"

Sitting down, hard, on a chair beside the bed as he laid back down, I cupped my head in my hands, my whole body shaking. Two nurses rushed in as my chest was heaving and tears busted through the dam, flood of emotions unstopped and raging. "This isn't fair! This isn't fair!" I yelled through sobs. "I cannot do more than two things at a time, I'm only human!"

Greg was raising his hand: "Praise God, let it out, baby! Praise God, this is so good for you to get it out!"

A nurse grabbed another chair and sat beside me, holding me and letting me cry and shout it out. "I have so.much.on.me! The house, Mom, Laura, worrying about Sam and Elli and Greg and Jacob! I cannot do this, I cannot, I'm not strong enough! *I'm not strong.enough!"*

"You don't have to be strong, Lovey," Greg said, tenderly, reaching for my hand. *My Greg was back!* His tender touch caused a new flood of tears and heaving, racking sobs. He said, "You can do all things, through Christ, Who gives *you* strength. It's not in your power, sweetheart, it's in Jesus. It's all Jesus, Terrie."

Believing the trauma-drama had been alleviated, the nurses left the room, leaving the door open, and calling the hospital's counseling staff to come and talk with me. Greg sat in his wheelchair in front of me, holding my hands. "I'm sorry, Terrie," he said. "I've been so preoccupied with trying to get better that I've neglected your needs. I am so sorry. Will you forgive me?"

"Yes," I said, a lone tear falling out of each red and puffy eye. "I'm sorry I freaked out."

"Nothing to apologize for," Greg said. "I forget that you and the kids are as much victims as I am."

We embraced, awkwardly, because of the wheelchair. Curiously, he looked up at the clock and sighed heavily. "Terrie," he sighed, "We have a meeting today, in a few minutes. It's with agents from the FBI."

"What?" I asked, perplexed. "Why?"

"They just want to talk about the case," he said. "Come on, let's go down."

The door into the meeting room was open, with several people already sitting around a conference table when I followed Greg as he rolled himself in the wheelchair. He sat at the head of the table with me to his right.

Introductions were made: a couple detectives from the Cabarrus County Sheriff's Department, and the rest were agents from the FBI. The FBI agent told us that there had been a viable threat against Greg's life. They told us that the gang in which the shooters were associated was exceedingly violent and vengeful; taking out witnesses was a defining trait. They didn't care who else they killed along with the witness.

I started to shake. It was all a bad dream; any moment now I'd wake up.

I actually pinched my arm in that meeting. I did not wake up; I was not asleep.

The agents went on describing other cases in which the gang had been involved. But, they said, they were there to help us. A guard would be posted on Greg's floor, near his door. A security detail would be monitoring the lobby and would also escort me back to my vehicle in the parking deck every night.

A Cabarrus County detective reached across and held my hand. She said, "I want to encourage you...the government has other ways to protect you."

One of the agents said, "You can enter the witness protection program."

Greg was unusually silent, even for him. I looked at him; he reached across and put his hand on my arm. "What...does that mean?" I asked the agent.

"We, meaning the federal government, would move you and your family to an undisclosed location, giving you new identities. New names, new jobs, new everything," the agent said, his chair squeaking as he shifted in his seat. "But, if you enter the program, you can never contact your friends and extended family again."

The full weight of the shooting, the horror of Greg's injuries, and the terror of what we were experiencing bore down upon me. I looked at Greg, still calm, and said, "What...what do we do?"

He smiled, ever so slightly. "Jesus. Jesus will protect us."

The detective across from me said, "Terrie. This gang is the most violent gang I've ever studied. The threat to your lives is real. Please, please—enter the program." She had tears in her eyes.

"Jesus," Greg said again. "Will protect us. Our God is more powerful than that gang."

The FBI agent cleared his throat. "The danger of something happening to your church is also very real."

That was the last straw. That was it. Sobbing, I pounded the table, saying "No!" over and over.

Greg reached over again and took my hand. "Even though I walk...through the shadow of death, I will fear no evil, for He is with us; His rod and His staff, they comfort us."

I looked at him; tears were brimming in his eyes but he was smiling. "This is a test," he whispered. "Do we trust Him?" I nodded.

Back in the room, Greg and I talked and we agreed that the developments warranted calling Pastor Ronnie. We hated to ask him to come to the hospital at that late hour, but we didn't want to tell him on the phone, as the FBI had told us not to tell anyone. But the immediate threat to the church, we felt, warranted telling our pastor.

Ronnie came to the hospital, sat on the bed, and listened intently as Greg told him what was going on. Ronnie prayed with us and counseled us biblically about God's protection. He said he would make some phone calls and have a representative from law enforcement stationed at the church every Sunday.

Ronnie's contact also made increased patrols of our neighborhood, to the point unmarked police cars were a constant presence near the house as people from church and the community at large worked on the renovations. Chris and some other people at the house carried licensed guns on their hips. Our home was safe.

After Ronnie had left, I thought about the meeting while I prepared Greg's clothes for the next day, placing them on his nightstand and gathering dirty clothes to take with me to wash. I commented to Greg about his quietness during the meeting.

"Come here," he said, stopping his transfer into the bed, which he patted. I sat down on the bed, and he took my hand. "They came yesterday to talk with me. Today was to tell you."

"What?" I asked.

"You remember the last night you spent at home? There was an unmarked police car outside, parked in front of the house. It left at daybreak. There have been unmarked police cruisers protecting our house every night."

The full weight of what he was telling me sunk in. I suddenly felt very small and scared, like a prairie dog hiding from a soaring hawk looking for a meal overhead.

"But, Terrie, look at it this way," he continued to hold my hands. "The Lord God, Commander of the Angel-Armies, is using those officers to protect us. He's got this. We trust Him."

That night, after walking to my car with an armed security guard, and winding my way through the parking deck, I found myself feeling small and puny. The meltdown I had had that morning over socks and a t-shirt seemed so far away.

The witness protection program: something you knew existed, but only in the context of bad mafia movies. I wasn't up to changing the identities of my family members and moving out west to become potato farmers in Idaho. I surely wasn't prepared to leave my church family.

I wasn't prepared for my church family to become victims in this, either.

Lord, God, I prayed aloud with the radio off. "I am not strong enough for this. But You are, Lord. Lead and guide us, please. I need *Your* strength, Lord. In Jesus' Name, Amen."

I flipped the radio on to WMIT 106.9 The Light, as usual. The last notes of "Same Power" by Jeremy

Camp were ending, then the night-time disk jockey said, "Someone needs to hear this tonight..."

My jaw dropped, I screamed, and I praised Jesus with everything I had: on the radio, Christian artist Matthew West was belting out his song "Strong Enough":

I know I'm not strong enough to be
Everything that I'm supposed to be
I give up
I'm not strong enough
Hands of mercy won't you cover me
Lord right now I'm asking you to be
Strong enough
Strong enough
For the both of us[2]

I knew right then, I was not to rely on my own strength but on His. It was all Jesus. Greg and I both were throwing ourselves at His blessed, pierced feet in total surrender. No, we would not cower before a group of thugs. We had the God of the Angel-

---

[2] ["Strong Enough," *The Story of Your Life* by Matthew West. Sparrow Records, October 5, 2010].

Armies covering us! Jesus, our Strength, our Rock, our King! He was—and is—strong enough.

Tensions were high after the law enforcement meeting. Each night after that, a security or police officer walked me to my car in the parking deck. A guard was stationed in the hallway outside Greg's door. Visitors had to use his alias, Donald Taylor, to gain access.

Once, though, Greg was showering with the help of his occupational therapist as I was folding clean clothes and placing them in the wardrobe's drawers, when there was a knock on the door. I did not recognize the small Asian lady before me, but it took me off guard when she asked, "Hello, is this Greg McKee's room?"

I looked quickly in the hall; the security guard must have stepped away. "Uhm...this is Donald Taylor's room."

"The man at the lobby told me this room was Greg's," she said, and moved to go in.

I am six feet tall. I am overweight. I am not a small woman. There was no way this lady was getting to my husband. Moving to block her way, I said in my pulpit voice, "You shall not pass."

Just then, the security guard ran down the hall from the men's restroom. He escorted her out. I called the nurse on the room phone while pulling my cell out of my back pocket to call the lead detective. Greg was oblivious to what had just happened. He was happily showering and scrubbing his armpits.

Within an hour, though, the hospital chief of security, the guard, two detectives, and two agents from the FBI had questioned the lady as well as the lobby guard, and we were all in another meeting room. The chief of security apologized profusely for the mistake and said the lady had been visiting her husband—another spinal patient—in rehab and had heard about our story from the news. Wanting to encourage us, she had asked the right questions of the wrong lobby security guard and had gained access.

The lobby security guard was moved to another department and replaced. The FBI agents were not impressed. They said that the gang the shooters were affiliated with often used people that no one would suspect, to do great harm. Anyone could be bought, they said. Everyone had a price.

That particular night I drove to Mom's in absolute fear. My stomach was in constant knots. Tensions were high. I prayed constantly. I knew God was with me; I also knew that satan had successfully planted a seed of fast-growing fear inside me that was being watered with every gun-toting escort to my car.

I called Greg one night from Mom's and told him that while our church family was keeping Mom and Laura well-stocked in food, that Mom needed to run some errands the next morning. I would be up later the next day.

The next morning, Mom, Laura, and I went to a large discount store to do some shopping. She had to get her medications from the pharmacy and some other things. We paid for the things in our carts and were walking back to the door, when a stocker accidentally dropped a large box of diapers right behind me. The loud sound the crashing box made when it hit the tile floor sounded just like the gun that had been used in the shooting.

Immediately, I screamed and fell to the floor. Shaking uncontrollably, sweating profusely, I experienced a full-on panic attack. Laura was crying; Mom was pleading with me to get up. "Let's go, Terrie, let's just go, it'll be okay."

The manager and the stocker helped us to the snack bar where we sat, trying to settle our nerves. Mom bought the three of us soft drinks. I reached in my purse, grabbed a familiar bottle, and swallowed two of my doctor's prescription calming pills as I held Laura. She was shaking. Mom explained to the very concerned manager; he immediately covered his mouth in horror. "I saw that on the news," he said. "Oh my gosh, I am so sorry."

As the manager and Mom talked, I sat there, thinking, *this is our new normal. Living in fear of the next bang. Living in fear of what will happen.*

A still, small voice broke through the noise of the fear and whispered, "For God has not given us a spirit of fear, but of power and of love and of a sound mind," (2 Timothy 1:7 KJV). If God has not given us a spirit of fear, I thought as I sipped my soda, "Then it's satan."

"Lord Jesus," I prayed quietly, as Laura held on to me and rubbed my cheek with her hand. I prayed for her as much as myself. "Please give us *Your* Spirit—one not of fear, but of power, and love, and a sound mind. Amen."

Amen.

Chapter Nine
Expecting

*When Jesus saw him lying there and learned that he
had been in this condition for a long time, he asked
him, "Do you want to get well?"*
John 5:6

Greg continued in physical and occupational
therapies at the hospital. A perfectionist by nature,
he needed structure—something in this new normal
where he felt out of control. He asked his therapists
the times in which he would be with them and wrote
those times down in a calendar he requested I bring
him. He held his therapists to that schedule, often
meeting them in the gym before they had a chance to
fetch him from his room.

He also found great comfort in the WMIT 106.9
The Light radio station's app he downloaded to his
phone. He would play Christian music, teachings,
and preaching in his room as he opened mail,
worked on schedules, or talked with visitors. Rehab
staff would comment his room was the most peaceful
in the place; he told them it was God's music playing.

Greg often involved me in his therapies in order that I would learn how to move him safely, how to transfer, or how to shower. Assisting him with daily tasks such as dressing, undressing, cooking, and even meal planning for paraplegics' delicate stomachs started in therapy sessions and classroom instructions.

Part of the education surrounding the new normal was what to do with our two cats, Henry and Rosie. At two years old, they were still feisty, and would often jump on people's laps. In an effort to minimize the risk associated with the possibility they could scratch Greg's legs, we made the decision to declaw them. One morning, I took them to our vet on the way to the hospital.

Greg was in physical therapy, learning how to roll over without the use of his legs, on top of a tall mat. My phone rang; it was the vet. I answered the phone on the way to the quiet hallway. "Hi," the vet said. "I have Henry on the table to do the surgery. We discovered that he has a heart murmur."

"Okay," I said. "What does that mean?"

"If we put him to sleep to do the surgery, he may not wake up."

I stared down the hallway. Henry was very much *my* cat. A big, strapping tom with long, charcoal gray fur, he was my *baby*.

The camel's back broke.

"Hold on," I squeaked through a waterfall of tears. So here was a choice: declaw Henry and face the possibility that he could die or face the possibility that he could scratch Greg and cause an infection, which would mean the potential amputation of a leg or death.

"Hold on, please," I said again, then I explained the situation to the vet.

She gasped; she had no idea about the seriousness of the decision she was asking me to make. I asked her to hold on one more minute; kneeling on the floor, I prayed and listened for wisdom from Jesus: *Sparrows, Terrie. Sparrows.*

I had heard Jesus' sweet voice as plainly as the vet's. Putting the phone to my ear, I said, "Operate. Please call me afterwards, no matter what."

"Absolutely," the vet said, hanging up.

I ran to Greg with wet and red eyes. He stopped rolling and sat up, with great difficulty. Margaret, his physical therapist, asked me what was wrong. I explained the situation to them, adding, "I told them to operate."

Greg patted beside himself on the mat. I sat down and fell into his arms. Margaret walked away to give us some privacy. "Abba Father," Greg prayed, "To others Henry may just be a cat. To us, Lord, he is family. Please, Lord, if it be Your will, preserve Henry's life. Help him during this time. Be with the vets and guide their hands. In Jesus' Name, Amen."

Peace flooded over me. Greg said, "He will be okay," as a tear brimmed out of his left eye and ran down his cheek.

Greg's therapy session was over, and according to his schedule, lunch would be soon. We went together to his room, and there were two lunch trays on the hospital table. He made excuse: "I ordered you lunch from the cafeteria! I wanted to eat with you."

He asked the blessing, and we ate quietly, both of us focused on Henry. We both jumped when my too-loud phone rang; "Hello?!" I exclaimed into the phone when I saw the vet's name on the screen.

"He made it!" the vet exclaimed; I could tell she had been crying. "Absolutely no problems. It's so weird—we tested him before the surgery, and there was a heart murmur. We tested him after the surgery—heart murmur. There was no murmur *during* the operation. It was just...*gone.*"

I burst into tears. "It's all Jesus!" I yelled and fell to laughing as we hung up.

Oh, Lord, how good You are! You, Lord, Who cares for Your children and Your creation! Lord Jesus, You are full of mercy, knowing we are so weak and cannot take another, single thing! Just when we're at the end of our rope, You, Oh Lord, are the Knot that prevents our fall! You are Peace, oh Jesus! You are Peace.

❧

Although Jacob had called me a few times a day when he first went back to school, his calls were getting fewer and farther between. I thought it was due to the stresses of being a music education major. But the night that Henry was discharged from the vet's office, and I was taking him to Mom's apartment to recuperate along with Rosie, Jacob called me. I could tell he had been crying.

"Mom," he said. "I am failing all my classes. I have done nothing except lie in bed, crying, since I got here. Mom, I just want to come home."

That all-to-familiar kick in the gut flared up again. I intentionally breathed in and out, flooded with emotions. "Jacob, baby boy, come on. Come on home."

"My finals..."

"Don't worry about them if you failing all your classes. Your mental, emotional, and spiritual health are more important than grades and classes. Do you need me to come help you?"

"No, I think I can get everything in the truck."

"Okay."

"Mom...are you mad?"

"No, Jacob," I said, using the most comforting and gentle voice I could muster. "I just want you home so I can hug you."

He burst into tears on the phone. I cried. He sobbed. Henry and Rosie meowed from the cat carriers. I turned the car off in the parking lot at Mom's apartment.

"Jacob," I asked, "When do you think you'll be here?"

"I'll pack tonight and leave sometime tomorrow. Mom...thank you."

"No, Jacob, thank you for telling me and being honest. I love you."

As the cats meowed pitifully, I sat in the relative quiet of my car while the sun set, and lifted Jacob, Sam, Elli, and Laura all up in prayer. I knew this was so hard on them all, but I didn't know what to do, other than pray—which was the most powerful thing I could do. After all, Jesus is so much bigger than any problem we face.

That night, as Mom snored from her bedroom and Laura slept on the air mattress beside me in the living room, I lay awake, thinking and praying. Experiencing a tragic event often means dealing with smaller traumatic situations that have been spawned from the initial event. The cumulative effect of all the little events on top of one another, while still reeling from the initial tragedy, is like walking through muddy oatmeal. It's hard and exhausting; everything sticks to you.

Yet—Jesus. I wondered at all the ways He had been there for us and marveled at the ways He met our needs even when we didn't know what they were.

Elroy. Suddenly, the man at the rest area who had helped Laura jumped in my mind and I bolted upright in bed. *Elroy. El Roi*, a Hebrew name of God, meaning "the God who sees me." I looked at my little girl, sleeping peacefully beside me, snuggling with her stuffed lamb, Betsy. "Lord Jesus," I prayed. "Thank you for seeing Laura's need to be comforted the night of the shooting. No wonder she went so easily to Elroy, Lord—it was an angel from You, Lord. You saw and You provided."

Lying back down, I turned my attention to the FBI meeting to process that, but instead lifted it in prayer. I clicked on a little lamp that was on the floor beside the air mattress and reached for my Bible beside the lamp. "You are my hiding place, oh Lord," I prayed Psalm 32:7 to Abba Father. "You will protect me from trouble and surround me with songs of deliverance..." Moving down the Psalm, I read verse 10: "Many are the woes of the wicked, but the Lord's unfailing love surrounds the one who trusts in him."

I meditated on verse 10. The Lord's unfailing love is not one of platitudes and empty comfort. It's an in-the-trenches, proactive, action verb. His unfailing love surrounds people who trust in Him. Yes, we had been through a lifetime of terrible things over the last couple of weeks, one on top of another. Yes, we were trying to unravel the whys and the hows of everything going on, but there was Jesus, surrounding us with His love and new-morning mercies every single day.

I turned in the Word of God to Lamentations 3:37-38 (NIV): "Who can speak and have it happen if the Lord has not decreed it? Is it not from the mouth of the Most High that both calamities and good things come?"

We don't like to think that God allows calamities, as the Scripture says, but we do want to think that God blesses us. Most people don't like rain, but they like the plants that benefit from it. Throughout Scripture, God called people back to Him. He used prophets, plagues, and problems to draw people to Him, as humanity doesn't tend to turn unless they're forced.

In the two weeks after the terrorist attacks of September 11, 2001, religious attendance (church, synagogue, temple) increased from 41% to 47%, then dropped back down to 41%)[3]. People who have experienced trauma tend to seek God; it's up to the Body of Christ, the Church, to preach the Gospel so that the visitors will go from seeking to salvation.

There are other people, however, who have their faith obliterated in the face of trials. They don't seek, they stew. Instead of being in the Bible, they dive into secular self-help books. They blame God while their hearts harden toward any mention of Him,

---

[3] "Religion in the Aftermath of September 11," Gallup News Service, Dec. 21, 2001. http://news.gallup.com/poll/5134/religion-aftermath-september.aspx

although they look to anything—people, drugs, sex, alcohol—for the peace they so desperately seek.

There is no peace outside of Christ, especially in trauma.

In John 6 we see Jesus visiting a pool called Bethesda, where a great number of disabled people would go to seek out the healing of an angel which supposedly stirred the waters. For 38 years a man had been an "invalid," Scripture tells us, and he would try to get to the water, but without the ability to walk or crawl, or someone to assist him, others would beat him to the stirred healing waters.

Enter Jesus, who saw the disabled man "lying there and learned that he had been in this condition for a long time, he asked him, "Do you want to get well?" Having turned to this passage as I lay awake that night, it was as though Jesus was asking me, "Do you want to get well?"

Not Greg, not Jacob or Laura, but He was pointing His finger at my exhausted, overwhelmed self, sitting on the edge of the pool and bemoaning the fact that Greg seemed to be swimming in Jesus' pool even as I was crawling to the waters, being pulled in every direction except poolside.

I was allowing the daily issues of everyday life, plus hospital visits, and my own internal struggles with post-traumatic stress disorder to pull me away from Jesus' healing. *Do you* want *to get well?*

"Yes," I said that night. "Lord Jesus, fill me with Your peace and restore to me the joy of Your salvation. In Your Name I pray, Amen."

I finally slept that night—the first time without reliving the shooting in my nightmares or seeing Greg belly-down on the floor, unable to get up.

Chapter Ten
Home for Christmas

The shepherds returned, glorifying and praising God for all the things they had heard and seen, which were just as they had been told.
Luke 2:20

Friends from church completed the house a few days before Christmas. They had moved and widened our bedroom door, created a larger, more useful closet, and turned the bathroom, which I disliked, into a spa-like room.

The former closet on the left going into the old bath became a perfect place for a sink and countertop, which Greg could roll under in his wheelchair. The former right closet became a place for a toilet with grab bars on the side walls.

The former three-piece bathroom was gutted, and gray tile applied on the walls and floor. New plumbing allowed for a hand-held shower on the right side and a regular shower-head for me on the left. The shower room was perfect; a hospital-provided shower bench for Greg completed it.

God used every bit of what I thought was incredibly bad bathroom design to create *exactly* what Greg and I needed in our post-shooting world. He wasted *nothing* in *His* plan for us—even in a bathroom.

New laminate hardwood throughout the house had replaced our dingy, worn carpeting. The old, inaccessible kitchen had been gutted to make a larger, modern farmhouse kitchen with stainless steel appliances and white cabinets.

The entire interior of the house had been freshly painted in a cream color—except for Laura's room. Laura had talked with Pastor Chris and requested a pink room, thank you very much, and he delivered.

A furniture store in Gastonia had extended a significant discount, and Ronnie and I had picked out a couch, chair, storage cabinet, bed for Jacob, and a new mattress and boxspring for Greg and I.

Chris had found a guy to make us a farmhouse dining table, and that would be delivered soon.

Friends and youth from church met Chris and I at the house, and we unloaded the storage unit. The goal was to get as much in order as possible in the house before Greg came home.

Gary and Barbara came down and were amazed at the transformation the house had experienced. All the pastors were at the house, finishing up some kitchen items, and they shared stories with Gary, Barbara, and I about how Jesus had orchestrated all aspects of the renovation—from providing all the funds, to bringing in companies in the community who donated materials and labor. A company in Charlotte built a brand-new, wheelchair accessible deck, huge and gorgeous, on the back of the house. A landscape company had donated plants and trees for updated landscaping around the deck and the front of the house. A ministry that builds ramps for disabled people built a ramp in the front of the house.

Chris had been in a big-box home improvement store, talking on the phone about the granite guy who couldn't do a quick-turnaround install for the kitchen countertops. A passer-by heard the conversation, and asked Chris if he, who had been on the news a good deal about the renovation, was the pastor helping the man who had been shot and his family.

This question made Chris nervous, but the guy went on to say that he cuts and installs kitchen countertops and would consider it an honor to do that *pro bono.*

Jesus.

It was amazing to hear our church family regale us with stories of how Jesus, ever the Carpenter, worked behind the scenes to prepare a home for us. Barbara was constantly dabbing tears of joy from her eyes while commenting that she was so very, very thankful.

I called Greg that night from the quiet solitude of the house. I walked throughout our home, telling him of everything that had been done. He cried.

The next day, with Jacob home and Elli on her way to spend Christmas with us, Barbara followed me to the hospital to pick Greg up.

Greg had been practicing getting in and out of the truck as part of therapy, and although the process was slow and cumbersome, and he was frustrated with himself, I reminded him that he was still new at this and it would come. Soon, I said, he would be transferring all by himself.

Barbara in her van and Greg and I in the truck pulled into the driveway at home. Mom, Gary, Laura, and Jacob ran out to greet him as he opened the door, saying, "Honey, I'm home!"

Medical gear and clothes from the hospital were unloaded from the vehicles as I helped Greg transfer to his wheelchair and pushed him up the ramp. The door was held open for him and he rolled in, looking around and saying, "Wow....it looks amazing. We have a whole new house!"

"Wow...we have a whole new bathroom!" he said, rolling into the master bath.

❧

In a small, dark apartment in Queens, New York, Terrell sat playing a video game. There was a pounding on the door, and the person with whom he and his wife were staying opened it. Suddenly, Terrell was being yanked from his game and thrown to the floor as a S.W.A.T. team from the New York Police Department handcuffed his wrists and read him his Miranda rights.

After a short stay at Riker's Island prison, he was extradited from New York to the Cabarrus County jail in North Carolina. He was caught.

Keyona too was arrested, for conspiracy to commit first-degree murder. The conspiracy came into play the moment she tried to make a three-way call to connect Darren with Terrell so Darren could order the hit from the jailhouse. This was a prime tactic used by their particular gang to intimidate and eliminate witnesses.

But Jesus.

The content of the attempted three-way call made it within the jurisdiction of the FBI, which triggered the use of technology to track Terrell's cell phone movements.

It was wonderful having Greg home. It was wonderful *being* home. Our LifeStudy class had given us a new Christmas tree and had decorated our home a few days before.

The Lord God had given us a whole new house, using His Church as His hands and feet to do so.

Jesus knew, a long time ago when Greg first walked in the house with his Realtor, that Greg would need those awkward bathroom closets to be made into a sink and toilet area, so the bathroom itself could be made into a shower room. Jesus took everything I hated about the bathroom and redeemed to make it accessible for Greg.

Jesus used the house renovation to bring a community together, and reuniting long-lost friends who volunteered for the project, unknowing the other had volunteered as well. He used a terrible event to show a lost and fallen community what His Bride is about: forgiving, sharing the Gospel, and helping those in need.

In many ways, we never came home after that fateful trip to Lynchburg for Thanksgiving. In a lot of other ways, we came home to better things. Yes, Greg is paralyzed. But because of the shooting, we were able to encounter Christ's awesome power, presence, and peace. Because of the experience we had in encountering Christ in trauma, I thank Him for the shooting.

Chapter Eleven
Through the Roof

When Jesus saw their faith, he said to the paralyzed man, "Son, your sins are forgiven."
Mark 2:5

∾

Jesus was teaching in a house. Overflowing crowds came from all over to hear Him, people jammed in the house, out the door, in the courtyard. It was standing-room only to hear the Preacher from Galilee.

There were four friends who had heard of Jesus and had heard of the miracles He had performed. These four friends had a fifth friend who was paralyzed, and spent his days lying on a mat. Day in, day out, this friend they cared so much about was reduced from a earning a viable wage to begging. It broke their hearts. Yet, in their little town, in a house of which they were familiar, Jesus was preaching. They picked up their friend's mat with him on it, knowing that if they could just get to Him, Jesus would heal their friend.

So they hoisted their friend up the exterior stairway and onto the roof, and began to tear away at the branches, mud, and thatch that made up that house's roof. They could hear Jesus' calm voice preaching inside, underneath their feet. They could also hear coughing and murmuring as people began to react to dried mud, dust, and sticks falling on them.

The hole was finally big enough to fit their friend's mat. Having had threaded ropes through holes they had made in each corner of the mat, they lowered the friend down, right in front of Jesus. The friend came to rest on the dirt floor at the feet of Jesus, and he looked up. Beyond Jesus' smiling face, in the hole, four faces peered in.

Total quiet. Jesus smiled. He looked up at the four faces peeking over the edge of the hole, then down at the man. "Son, your sins are forgiven."

Murmuring. Outright gasps. Jesus looked over near the door, where a small group of Pharisees and teachers of the Law were jammed in together. His brow furrowed, and He looked at one particular teacher. "Why are you thinking these things? Which is easier: to say to this paralyzed man, 'Your sins are forgiven,' or to say, 'Get up, take your mat and walk'? But I want you" Jesus pointed to the teacher, who had his mouth hanging open, "to know that the Son of Man has authority on earth to forgive sins."

Jesus looked down at the man, who had been looking at the door too. The man looked up at Jesus, whose brown eyes twinkled at him. "I tell you," He said, reaching His hand down, "Get up, take your mat and go home."

The four friends up top starting smacking each other's shoulders as their friend sat up, grabbed Jesus' hand, and with Jesus' carpenter-strong arm pulling, stood up. Gasps. Merriment. General shock and amazement overtook the crowd, who started pointing at the man and at Jesus, saying, "We have never seen anything like this!" [Mark 2:1-12 NIV, emphasis and storytelling added].

Why did Jesus forgive the friend of his sins *before* He healed his physical condition? The man's physical condition enabled the man to get a front-row seat at the feet of Jesus. His physical condition, fueled by his friends' faith, enabled him to encounter Jesus' power, presence, and peace in the middle of a surging crowd. Yet, Jesus decided to use the man's disability to reach his heart first.

Having a disability of faith is much worse than a physical disability. A person who has no faith in Christ, does not know Him as Lord and Savior, is worse off than someone who has a physical or intellectual disability.

Greg's faith in God, while strong, grew exponentially after he was shot. Lying there on that cold tile floor, blood dripping from his face, he encountered the very power, presence, and peace of Christ even has the rest stop was swirling with people. Christ used his shooting to not just reach a community, but to reach Greg.

I had prayed several months before that Jesus would humble Greg, who was having an issue with pride. I prayed that Christ would grow Greg's faith. Although

I had no idea Jesus would use an attempted armed robbery to do that, "we know that in all things God works for the good of those who love him, who have been called according to his purpose," (Romans 8:28 NIV).

For an unbeliever who experiences violent trauma such as what we experienced, life is no better than what it is. They are paralyzed, or an amputee, or have some other disability. Life is hard, just as life is hard when you're a wheelchair-bound believer, but the difference is this: when they die, they are doomed to spend eternity in hell.

Yet, because Jesus took our sins upon Himself at the cross and died doing so, we have remission of sins. There is no other way to have remission of sins except through the blood of the Lamb, Jesus Christ. Accepting His atoning gift of grace on the cross, acknowledging Him as Lord, is the only way to gain salvation.

When, three days later, Christ arose from a borrowed tomb, He defeated death. He conquered it. This means that not even death has power over a follower of Jesus.

So, when a believer experiences violent trauma such as Greg did, and has some sort of physical disability because of it, that disability is a temporary condition. Peter wrote, "I think it is right to refresh your memory as long as I live in the tent of this body, because I know that I will soon put it aside, as our Lord Jesus Christ has made clear to me," (2 Peter 1:13-14 NIV.) Tents, in that nomadic culture, were temporary structures, made for passing through locations on the way to more fertile soil for livestock. Peter compares our earthly bodies with these temporary structures as something to be used while we're passing through this world, with our eyes focused on what is ahead for the believer of Jesus Christ: heaven.

Experiencing a violent trauma is not the worst thing that can happen. Being paralyzed or otherwise physically disabled is not the worst thing that can happen. Because of Christ, not even *death* is the worst thing that can happen, because He defeated death!

Glory!

Revelation 21:3-5 states this incredible reminder of Christ's power, presence, and peace: "And I heard a loud voice from the throne saying, 'Look! God's dwelling place is now among the people, and he will dwell with them. They will be his people, and God himself will be with them and be their God. He will wipe every tear from their eyes. There will be no more death or mourning or crying or pain, for the old order of things has passed away.' He who was seated on the throne said, 'I am making everything new!' Then he said, 'Write this down, for these words are trustworthy and true.'"

This passage gives us a crystal-clear picture of what heaven will be like for those who follow Jesus: the paralyzed will walk, the blind will see, we will all have brand-new resurrection bodies which will not ache or have arthritis. There won't even be pimples in heaven! The two babies I miscarried, Emma Elyse and Matthew Dean, I will be able to hold! But more than that, we will see *Jesus*!

It is just amazing, thinking about this. The same Jesus who looked down with compassion at the paralyzed man on the floor, forgave his sins and healed him, is the same Jesus who sat on the floor with Greg at that rest stop, protected me as I walked back and forth to the parking deck, and pricked the hearts of men and women all over the world to pray for us and give money so that our home could become wheelchair accessible. *Jesus* did all this, using His children as the vessels through which His mercy and grace were poured.

This same Jesus wants to have a relationship with *you*. He wants a deeper relationship with *you*. The God of the Universe is not an impersonal god who sits up there somewhere on a throne and looks down on us. No, He sent His Son Jesus, who sent the Comforter, the Holy Spirit, to be with us in each aspect of our lives. He doesn't want ten percent of our lives, friends. He wants His children to love Him with "*all* your heart and with *all* your soul and with *all* your strength," (Deuteronomy 6:5 NIV, emphasis added).

He wants all of us so that when tragedies do strike—and they will—we are better prepared spiritually to have faith in Him that He will provide for us, whatever the need. Being close to Christ *before* trauma helps us *in* trauma. Being *in* the Word helps us to *remember* and *share* the Word when tragedy strikes.

In order to have the peace that passes all understanding even in trauma, friends, we have to have a relationship with Jesus Christ, the Prince of Peace, before trauma.

Chapter Twelve
That My Heart Will Sing Your Praises

*You turned my wailing into dancing; you removed
my sackcloth and clothed me with joy,
that my heart may sing your praises and not be silent.
Lord my God, I will praise you forever.*
Psalm 30:11-12

୧

After Greg came home from the hospital, God did the most amazing things, astounding the medical team that worked with him in the hospital and in outpatient physical therapy. Within two weeks of coming home, he made the decision to come off all narcotic pain medications.

He had promised to coach basketball in the church's recreation department for 4-5 year olds, and he kept that promise, a month after coming home. Despite being in great pain during practices and games, the determination he showed the kids he coached taught them much more than dribbling and shooting baskets.

Within 100 days of the shooting, with me driving him, Greg went back to work as a dispatcher for a chemical transportation company. The non-narcotic pain medication he was taking for severe nerve pain dulled him mentally, and to do the best job for the company which had supported him and us through the shooting and hospital stay, he made the intentional decision to decrease the dosage. He learned non-medication methods to deal with the pain.

He took driving lessons to learn how to operate hand controls, as he was determined to drive himself. So over the course of about four sessions, he mastered driving with hand controls. There was enough money left over from the house renovation from the crowdfunding to buy a four-door sedan that he could get into by himself. He tested several models, transferring into the drivers' seat, taking his wheelchair apart, maneuvering the chair across the steering wheel and to the passenger seat. Finally, the car he had wanted in the first place became the car that fit the most. He named it "Buggy."

On April 6, 2016, he kissed me goodbye, rolled down the ramp, to the car, transferred in, took the wheelchair apart, moved it to the passenger seat, and drove to work—*all by himself.* Most people just get up, get dressed, get in the car, and drive to work. Greg does all those things too, only it involves so much more and with incredible pain besides.

In the fall, almost to the first-year anniversary of the shooting, Greg and our friend Lisa completed his first ever 5K in Charlotte. He wanted to do it to prove to himself he could do it—and in his everyday wheelchair, with a special wheel (donated by our friend Rick) attached to the front to elevate the front casters, he pushed and pushed himself, with encouragement (and a little pushing) from Lisa, he did it. He didn't finish first—but he didn't finish last, either.

Greg is an avid sports enthusiast, especially when it comes to his beloved Buckeyes of his alma mater, The Ohio State University, and the Cincinnati Reds. He had played baseball in high school, and had coached t-ball, basketball, and soccer for our church. It was no surprise to me, then, after meeting a young lady and her dad at the 5K who had told him about the wheelchair basketball team she was on, that he wanted to find out more about it.

After his first practice of the Charlotte Rollin' Hornets' D3 team, he was hooked. Even though he didn't have a special basketball wheelchair and practiced in his everyday chair, he would go and practice, and practice *hard*. Pounds started rolling off him.

The team located a donated chair and gave it to him, and that only solidified his drive to practice, learn to shoot better, and improve his chair skills. Wheelchair basketball, to the spectator, is a violent sport, but he loves it.

Darren eventually pled guilty to all charges, and he was given 23 years in the North Carolina prison system.

Terrell pled not guilty and his trial was held in December 2017. Keyona turned state's evidence and testified against Terrell. Most of the inside details about Darren and Terrell's actions for this book were gleaned from the trial.

Terrell was found guilty on all counts and was sentenced to 27 years in the state's prison system. Darren and Terrell are not in the same prison, which, given their history with gangs, is a good thing.

Terrell's profanity-laced conversation was "accidentally" found by a detective during his trial, after spending hours listening to recordings. It was a key factor in the jury's decision to find him guilty on all counts. It is still not known how that cell phone app, which Terrell had used to record himself rapping, suddenly turned on at the exact moment he began telling his friend about his involvement in Greg's shooting.

Jesus.

Keyona was released with time served for her part in testifying against Terrell. Greg and I both pray for her, and her two children, that she will turn to Jesus and get her life back on track.

Jacob left WCU and has battled depression on and off since the shooting. He is now getting his groove back and is enjoying working at a local theme park. He was recently promoted to an aquatics supervisor.

Laura has struggled with remembering her daddy before the shooting. Diagnosed with dyslexia in the first grade, she struggles with reading, but has improved this year with special classes and tutoring.

Sam moved out of the group home, and back in with us. It's been an adjustment, but he is much happier home than he was away. Elli moved in with us after her first year of college. She is doing well as an online college student and is working part-time.

The Lord has blessed us with the testimony He has given us and He has opened up doors of ministry because and through the shooting. Because of his testimony, Greg has been afforded the opportunity to share the Gospel with people who have disabilities. The Lord has blessed me with open doors and opportunities that have launched my speaking and writing career—all to glorify Him.

I would be amiss if I did not add this: Jesus increased my faith through this trauma. In the years since though, with many people commenting on what a strong faith "I" had, Jesus poked me *hard* and whispered that it was faith in *Him*—not my faith, but faith in *Him*—that was most important. Our faith can quickly descend into an idol, especially if we start listening to people who are amazed by actions of obedience and trust to Christ.

There were times throughout the shooting, the immediate aftermath, and in the years since that brought me to my knees, and not in prayer. The sheer weight of the pounding onslaught of information and terror and juggling life can quickly weigh a person down. How do you manage that in tangible ways as a person of faith?

By leaning on Christ. Praying without ceasing. Diving into and staying in the Word of God. Surrounding yourself with prayer warriors and people of faith who will not only lift you in prayer, but deliver meals, drop everything and come to the hospital, and hold you when you ugly-cry—all without saying trite clichés as a way to "comfort."

Friends, even in the midst of trauma, God is so good. Often we can see His goodness in the rear-view mirror, looking back on how He was there for us *in the midst* of it all. Yet, in His sovereignty, Jesus *prepares* us to lean on Him during the trauma, way before it actually happens.

For example, Sam usually would go in the same restroom with Greg when we'd travel before he was in the group home. Sam entered residential living 21 *days* prior to the shooting. Had Sam been in the restroom with Greg the night of the shooting, we'd be looking at a whole other tragedy.

The spring prior to the shooting, I had completed Stephen's Ministry[4] training to become a lay minister to comfort and disciple others during times of great need. Think about that. Instead of God using that training so that I could minister to others, Christ

---

[4] Stephen's Ministry training available through Stephen Ministries Saint Louis, www.stephenministries.org. *Stephen Ministry Training Manual,* Stephen Ministries, 2000.

Himself used that training to minister to me. I couldn't see it while Greg was in the hospital and rehab, but I started remembering things about the training when he was home. Things like the course of a crisis, the stages of grief, actively listening, dealing with feelings. It was because of the Stephen's Ministry training that I knew I had PTSD and needed help—and step on it. God in His wisdom knew I would need that information and He used the training in which I participated in to get that information to me.

Even now, with the writing of this book and subsequent speaking engagements, Christ is opening up doors of ministry that He had ordained for Greg and I, because of the trauma we experienced on November 28, 2015. God doesn't waste anything.

John 12:32 states, "And I, when I am lifted up from the earth, will draw all people to myself." When Jesus is lifted up, whether in word or deed, through tragedy, trauma, or illness, He will use those testimonies to draw people to Him. What a glorious

opportunity to worship Jesus, by lifting Him up to others who need Him.

Greg's shooting was horrific, and we have days that are just downright hard. It's still difficult to see Greg in a wheelchair when I remember what he was like before. It's even more difficult when Laura asks me, "Mommy, will Daddy ever walk again?"

When I answer her, I breathe deep, close my eyes, and reply, "Yes, Laura, yes. He will walk in heaven—all because of Jesus."

Chapter Thirteen
Remember

Remember the wondrous works that he has done,
his miracles, and the judgments he uttered...
Psalm 105:5

At the time of this writing, it has been over seven years since Greg was shot and paralyzed. As the days became weeks then grew steadfastly into months, we kept reminding each other that although we didn't know what we were doing—yet. But we were learning.

As months became years, we finally found a rhythm to the days and nailed down certain aspects of Greg's home care: the careful placement of travel pillows under his left leg and both feet to prevent pressure sores and increase blood circulation when he slept was a huge accomplishment. Discovering that a standard pillow, placed on its long end at the end of his feet, held the covers above his toes so they wouldn't develop pressure sores, too. All this was trial-and-error; it's not taught in the hospital or in the spinal cord injury notebook.

That notebook is in the top shelf of our closet. It hasn't been touched in six and a half years. I'll probably donate it at some point.

Laura

After the shooting, we were very much encouraged to put her into public school, as her education was deemed by some to be "too much" for me with "all of Greg's care, too." This was a decision that always pained both Greg and I—and eventually, made me mad at myself for listening to that counsel. She was in public school for the remainder of kindergarten and all of first through second grade.

We were told, at the end of second grade, that she wasn't on grade level with reading and to hold her back a year. Instead, we pulled her from public school and homeschooled her—and have been doing so ever since (she is now in the seventh grade). By Christmas of her third-grade year, she was reading on grade level.

In early 2016, she and I were talking about how Jesus brought us through the shooting and all that He was doing. On a warm winter day, sitting on our porch swing, I had the ultimate privilege of leading her to the Lord. She was baptized a couple weeks later by Pastor Chris. Her faith is strong and is ever growing.

I found, homeschooling Laura, that resources for homeschooling *just one child* was extremely hard to come by. While at a blogging conference, I had the revelation that if I can't find resources—create them. So, I launched my new website, Homeschooling1Child.com, in the summer of 2018. It's been a blast, speaking and sharing our testimony in various forms (the shooting *always* comes up) at homeschool conventions. I've made some incredible friends along the way, too.

Charlotte Rollin' Hornets

Greg has continued to play for the wheelchair basketball team, the Charlotte Rollin' Hornets. The team's donated chair gave way to a chair that was measured to Greg's exact dimensions and custom-built for him, thanks to a grant from the Challenged Athletes Foundation.

Greg playing wheelchair basketball has given us the opportunity to travel to places like Alabama, Florida, throughout the Carolinas, Tennessee, Kentucky, and as far as Wichita, Kansas for the national wheelchair basketball championships—multiple times. Because of homeschooling, we can take Laura and do some roadschooling, taking time to stop at historical places to widen her sphere of learning.

Greg's dedication to basketball practices and learning plays paid off. Greg is now a starter for the Rollin' Hornets, but his competitive nature doesn't stop on a basketball court, but is extended to tennis courts, too. He plays wheelchair tennis with a group in Charlotte—and has a wicked forearm that is gaining a reputation. Ironically, playing tennis has drastically improved his chair handling skills for basketball.

Cancer

On February 18, 2021, my worst fears since the shooting came to fruition—Greg called me on the way to work one morning, saying he had been in a car wreck.

He had been in the center turning lane, to turn left into his work's driveway, when a speeding car attempted to pass him on the left—hitting Buggy's front left quarter-panel, destroying its axle, and throwing Greg and his car into a 360. Buggy was totaled.

I immediately drove to his work and took him home—he had denied medical help at the scene—but he seemed...*off.* After he couldn't remember certain facts (like his phone number) and complaining of a headache (which was unusual), I drove him to the hospital in Charlotte. A CT scan showed he had a mild concussion—and an abnormally enlarged thyroid.

Once again, here was an opportunity to yield to God's grace and pour out prayers to Him. We remembered the ways in which He had shown Himself to us with the shooting, and we knew Jesus was in the fire with us. Tests, blood work, imaging, and biopsies all confirmed the worst: my beloved, who had already been through so much in five years, had cancer.

Surgery was scheduled. Prayers lifted. Almighty God, Who heard prayers from us, family, and friends, answered with a successful operation which removed the entire thyroid, all the cancer, with clean margins, besides. Oh, He is so good! Yes, Greg must be on thyroid medication for the rest of his life, but it's a small price to pay when one thinks of the alternative.

Here's the miracle part of Greg's cancer diagnosis: had it not been for the car wreck, Greg would have never had that enlarged thyroid checked out. For someone who's paraplegic, he really hates going to the doctor. He stopped going to the spinal doctor in late 2016, deeming it pointless because there would be no change in his paralysis. Our primary care doctor handles any urinary tract infections that come up, but they are few and far between.

It's wondrous how Christ works. Romans 8:28 states, "And we know that in all things God works for the good of those who love him, who have been called according to his purpose." Had it not been for that horrific car wreck, Greg would have never been checked out, and the thyroid cancer that lay growing would have metastasized—and life would have changed yet again for Greg and our family. I am *so very grateful* for that car wreck, as God forced the issue and *made* His stubborn, anti-medical son get examined. It was only through the CT scan, originally done for the concussion, that the thyroid tumor was flagged.

So many times in life we think that bad things happen to us for no reason, but in hindsight, those same bad things held the keys to doors that we would have never opened ourselves. Growth in faith in Christ often comes through trials, not times of blessings. Let us lean into Christ during times of woe and hardship, and ask Him: *what are You teaching me through this?*

Jacob

Jacob had some issues relating to the shooting, but he's worked through them. He didn't go back to college, but instead found his calling in theme park operations and management. He met the love of his life, Allyssa, and they married in October 2021. Greg had tied every tie Jacob had worn, so it was touching that Jacob asked him if Greg would tie his wedding tie, as well. In the months leading up to the wedding, Greg went to physical therapy, ordered a set of locking braces for his legs, and learned how to stand using a walker—all to stand at eye-level and tie Jacob's tie.

There wasn't a dry eye around.

Allyssa has been a blessing to him and, indeed, all of us. They live out of state, now, and although we don't see them nearly enough, we keep in touch as much as possible.

Sam

Sam left the group home a year after the shooting and came home. He wanted his *own space*, and not in a group home, so in May 2020 availability came open in an apartment complex for elderly and disabled people. He moved in, decorated it, and has been doing relatively well. He still visits, mainly to do his laundry and use our Internet, but he always does some chore for me. He's moved mulch, helped tend the small flock of chickens we acquired, and done other things to help me.

Elli

Elli married in 2018, and while she walked herself down the aisle for many reasons other than her dad's inability to do so, he did surprise her at the reception, which was in an event barn. Using a safety harness and ropes, with a lot of muscular men to help hoist him up, he did in fact get to dance with his beloved daughter on her wedding day.

There wasn't a dry eye around.

Elli is now in the process of a divorce, but she has grown so much in the years of her marriage. I'm so very proud of her, learning who she is, and has grown into an incredibly responsible, giving, and compassionate woman. She and I have grown very close over the last five years especially and am proud to call her my daughter.

We don't do step- or half- anything. They're all our kids.

Faithfulness

We don't say, "God is faithful." Of course, He is—
the Bible promised that! The issue is, are *we* faithful,
as believers? Do we worship and praise despite the
things happening in our lives? Do we call out to
Him, and lean on Him for understanding?

This story about a family stopping at a rest area only
to have their lives jumbled upside-down is not about
us. It's about Christ's power, peace, and presence
that hasn't ended. He has answered prayers big and
small—a new car (Buggy 2.0) for Greg, a growing
ministry in which we help other families affected by
paralysis and trauma, and tangibly seeing the effects
of God's hand.

Over the last seven years, God has been so protective
of me with the PTSD I developed after the shooting,
and has helped me manage severe anxiety. Christians
are not immune to anxiety, and it has nothing to do
with the amount they pray, either. We're human,
and things happen in our lives that are so incredibly
huge and difficult that it messes with us,
psychologically. Jesus did not fault the blind man for

his disability, but reached down, spit in the dirt, and used a mud ointment on the man's eyes. John 9:7 (NIV) tells us that Jesus said, "Go…wash in the Pool of Siloam" (this word means "Sent"). So the man went and washed, and came home seeing." Perhaps the mud had nothing to do with the healing, but it was the man's obedience to Jesus' command to wash it off that did.

Breathing exercises, medication, and prayer has helped my anxiety greatly. Closing my eyes when Greg drives us through Atlanta to get to basketball tournaments helps a lot, too. But if I neglected to do my breathing exercises, take my meds, or not pray, then I am being disobedient in not utilizing the tools Jesus has given me to help me through this season.

It's all Jesus, friends. It's because of Him my beloved husband is alive today, my family is doing well, and He is using the story He gave us for His glory.

It can't get better than that.

Chapter Fourteen
Addendum

Posts from NearYourAltar.com

My Statement at the Sentencing of My Husband's Shooter

October 26, 2017

The sentencing hearing for the man, Darren, who shot my husband at a rest stop after Thanksgiving 2015 was held on October 26, 2017. I had the opportunity to read the following victim impact statement to the judge in the courtroom with the defendant, his attorney, the assistant district attorney, sheriff deputies and other people present.

Your Honor,

My name is Terrie McKee. I am the wife of the victim. But that is not exactly true. Greg, myself, and our whole family were victims of the shooting on November 28, 2015 which left my husband paralyzed from the waist down.

It has been almost two years since a stop for a

restroom break changed our lives forever. The defendant's actions and choices that day have created undue hardship on our whole family.

We were having a difficult time financially before the shooting; now, because of the paralysis, we are desperately struggling financially. Because of the paralysis, Greg's bladder and bowels no longer function as they should, so he has to constantly wear incontinence pads and briefs to catch the leaking urine. These are not cheap. The catheters that are required for him to urinate because of the paralysis from the shooting are an added cost we did not have before. The maintenance on his wheelchair and the need he has for a standing frame – all of these are things he requires but we cannot afford. They are not covered by insurance.

His medications, and my medications for anxiety and depression are direct results of the shooting on November 28.

Your Honor, we live less than paycheck-to-paycheck and are nearly always within one month from losing everything. It was tight before – in fact, the only thing that was in Greg's wallet the night of the shooting was his grocery cart quarter – but now, finances are beyond tight.

While we are grateful to God for His provision, we have to make the conscious decision to either purchase the medical supplies he needs or do without some item of food, car repair, or clothing for our children. Although we are certainly thankful to our church family and community for renovating our home to accommodate Greg's wheelchair; the fact is, because of our large family, we need a larger home. It's not a want; it's a need. Yet, because of medical bills, ongoing medical requirements, bulky medical equipment that takes up a ton of space, and the inability for Greg to make more money because of being paraplegic, we cannot afford a larger house. This is a constant source of emotional stress – to know you need something but cannot get it, because your husband was shot and paralyzed in a random crime event.

The shooting caused me, personally, to have PTSD

very similar to a soldier who has fought in war. Car backfires, or someone dropping a box, the sight and sounds of an ambulance – all cause me to have severe panic attacks. The thought that a severe urinary tract infection or an infected pressure sore can take the life of my husband at any given time creates daily anxiety.

The choice the defendants made that night to shoot my husband has forever changed our family.... I have a tremendously difficult time staying home by myself. Driving up I-85 and seeing the rest stop sign sends me into a full-on anxiety attack. I have had panic attacks so bad they have sent me to the hospital.

It is extraordinarily painful experiencing the love of my life cry out with searing nerve pain and being unable to do anything about it. Paraplegia requires that I help him shower, get dressed and undressed, and even assist him in moving his bowels. He is 45 years old – this is our life now, for as long as he lives, because he was shot by the defendant.

Greg's career choices and ability to make more

money to support his family, and his medical needs, have been diminished greatly and forever because of the inability to stand. Since I am also the caregiver for our autistic son and little girl who suffers with chronic migraines, I cannot work outside the home. Greg is the only breadwinner. The ADA and equal opportunity programs are great but one has to be physically able to do a job. He cannot find better-paying employment because of the paralysis due to the shooting.

The shooting not only destroyed his vertebrae, but it shattered our whole family's hopes, dreams, and aspirations. It has affected each of our children.

Our son who witnessed the shooting had to leave Western Carolina and his dream of being a high school band director. He has battled depression because of the shooting.

Our son who has autism is angry and hurt that someone would do this to his stepfather. Because of his disability, he doesn't fully understand – but he constantly blames me for the shooting because I had to use the bathroom. Can you imagine what emotional trauma this does to me?

Our oldest daughter will not have the opportunity to have her Daddy walk her down the aisle in a year or two when she gets married. We all grieve this. The Daddy-Daughter dance she has dreamt about will not be able to happen.

Our little girl, the youngest, also witnessed the shooting. She saw her Daddy in his own blood, crying out thinking he was dead. She constantly asks if he will ever walk again. She has decided she wants to be a surgeon when she grows up, so she can get the bullet out of his back.

The shooting has affected us in other ways, Your Honor. Most people who see us at church or in public see us as strong and resilient. In reality, we are suffering and hurting. It's awfully hard to talk about a tragedy and trauma of this magnitude—who has that kind of experience? We feel so very alone. We are struggling in every way. Yet, Jesus is with us and we know that He is our Provision, our Peace, and our

Protector. In His strength, we will move forward the best we can.

≈

The defendant received 23 years in prison. In NC, there are six record levels in the felony punishment chart -- the higher the number, the more violent the offender. The defendant is a level four offender with 11 points for prior convictions over ten years, starting at age sixteen when he dropped out of school. The week before the hearing, he claimed he was "disrespected" by his cellmate, whom he subsequently beat up. He was in solitary confinement because of the beating during the hearing. He will be 51 years old when he leaves prison. No one from his family showed at the hearing.

From https://www.nearyouraltar.com/blog/my-statement-at-the-sentencing-of-my-husbands-shooter

What I told the Man Who Shot My Husband at His Sentencing

January 9, 2018

The 12-day trial of one of the men, Terrell, responsible for shooting and paralyzing my husband Greg ended just a few days before Christmas. After approximately a three-hour deliberation, the jury found the defendant guilty on all charges. The judge sentenced him to 23 years in a North Carolina state prison. At his sentencing, immediately after the jury's verdict was read, I was given the opportunity to say a statement on behalf of my family and I. This is that statement.

Your Honor, the past two years have been the hardest of our lives. Not only have Greg and I, and our children, have had to deal with the physical, emotional, and mental ramifications, but our family and friends have been affected as well.

The two defendants in the shooting...will eventually be released from prison. They will go about their lives. Meanwhile, my husband will be in a wheelchair —paralyzed—for his entire life.

The dreams we had before November 28, 2015—to have a working farm, to provide respite for families of special needs children, to welcome our home to foster children—were shattered because of the shooting. We are still trying to wrap our heads around what the Lord would have us do in this season of pain and struggle.

Although (the defendants) left empty-handed the night of the shooting does not mean they did not steal from us. Because of Greg's medical needs, wheelchair maintenance, and a sharp increase in doctor co-pays—every time we have to spend money on his paraplegia, it's as though (they) are stealing from us time and time and time again. We are not wealthy, your Honor. We exist on Greg's income which, frankly, is not enough to cover the normal family expenses plus his medical needs. Our oldest son has autism and lives at home, which means I am his caregiver as well as Greg's and am unable to work.

Yet, your Honor, in just a week, we will celebrate the birth of Jesus Christ, who came to this earth as a baby to die for our sins and to be raised to life so that we too may live.

In that spirit, Your Honor, in the power of Jesus Christ the Son of the Living God, we forgive (them) for what they did to us. We forgive them. They still must deal with the ramifications of the shooting, like we have to, every single day. But in the name of Jesus, we forgive them.

It is our fervent prayer that they will seek out a prison chaplain and ask about salvation in Jesus Christ, for it is only through Jesus that they will know peace. Not through stealing, not through gangs, not through crime—but only through Jesus Christ.

Your Honor, thank you for this time to speak before the court. Merry Christmas.

In North Carolina, convicted criminals do not receive time off for good behavior; instead, they have

time added for bad behavior. At the time of this writing, both Darren and Terrell are up to 30 years each—mainly for gang-related activities.

About the Author

"Though the mountains be shaken and the hills be removed, yet my unfailing love for you will not be shaken nor my covenant of peace be removed," says the LORD, who has compassion on you.
Isaiah 54:10

Terrie Bentley McKee is a Christian author, speaker, and blogger at Homeschooling One Child and Near Your Altar. Terrie encourages Christians all over the world to live a life worthy of the calling of Christ Jesus. Married to Greg with a blended family of four children, the Lord has blessed her with a wide variety of testimonies to encourage others in the walk of Jesus Christ. Terrie and her family call North Carolina home. When she isn't teaching life skills to her son with autism, writing, speaking, or wrangling a huge dog, several cats, and a flock of chickens, she can be found napping on the couch or enjoying a nice cup of hot tea. She has most recently discovered an intense fondness for snorkeling but not of sharp coral.

Terrie is always available to speak at churches, retreats, conferences, revivals, or community organizations that help the differently-abled population, women who are or have been in domestic violence situations, or caregiving.

Thank you for reading.

For booking information, contact Terrie at homeschooling1child.com or nearyouraltar.com.

www.ingramcontent.com/pod-product-compliance
Lightning Source LLC
Chambersburg PA
CBHW051519120626
46551CB00012B/1000